I0003591

Contents

What Is Amazon Kinesis Data Streams?

Use Amazon Kinesis Data Streams to collect and process large streams of data records in real time.

You'll create data-processing applications, known as *Amazon Kinesis Data Streams applications.* A typical Amazon Kinesis Data Streams application reads data from a *Kinesis data stream* as data records. These applications can use the Kinesis Client Library, and they can run on Amazon EC2 instances. The processed records can be sent to dashboards, used to generate alerts, dynamically change pricing and advertising strategies, or send data to a variety of other AWS services. For information about Kinesis Data Streams features and pricing, see Amazon Kinesis Data Streams.

Kinesis Data Streams is part of the Kinesis streaming data platform, along with Amazon Kinesis Data Firehose. For more information, see the Amazon Kinesis Data Firehose Developer Guide. For more information about AWS big data solutions, see Big Data. For more information about AWS streaming data solutions, see What is Streaming Data?.

What Can I Do with Kinesis Data Streams?

You can use Kinesis Data Streams for rapid and continuous data intake and aggregation. The type of data used includes IT infrastructure log data, application logs, social media, market data feeds, and web clickstream data. Because the response time for the data intake and processing is in real time, the processing is typically lightweight.

The following are typical scenarios for using Kinesis Data Streams:

Accelerated log and data feed intake and processing
You can have producers push data directly into a stream. For example, push system and application logs and they are available for processing in seconds. This prevents the log data from being lost if the front end or application server fails. Kinesis Data Streams provides accelerated data feed intake because you don't batch the data on the servers before you submit it for intake.

Real-time metrics and reporting
You can use data collected into Kinesis Data Streams for simple data analysis and reporting in real time. For example, your data-processing application can work on metrics and reporting for system and application logs as the data is streaming in, rather than wait to receive batches of data.

Real-time data analytics
This combines the power of parallel processing with the value of real-time data. For example, process website clickstreams in real time, and then analyze site usability engagement using multiple different Kinesis Data Streams applications running in parallel.

Complex stream processing
You can create Directed Acyclic Graphs (DAGs) of Amazon Kinesis Data Streams applications and data streams. This typically involves putting data from multiple Amazon Kinesis Data Streams applications into another stream for downstream processing by a different Amazon Kinesis Data Streams application.

Benefits of Using Kinesis Data Streams

While you can use Kinesis Data Streams to solve a variety of streaming data problems, a common use is the real-time aggregation of data followed by loading the aggregate data into a data warehouse or map-reduce cluster.

Data is put into Kinesis data streams, which ensures durability and elasticity. The delay between the time a record is put into the stream and the time it can be retrieved (put-to-get delay) is typically less than 1 second — in other words, a Amazon Kinesis Data Streams application can start consuming the data from the stream almost immediately after the data is added. The managed service aspect of Kinesis Data Streams relieves you of the operational burden of creating and running a data intake pipeline. You can create streaming map-reduce type applications, and the elasticity of Kinesis Data Streams enables you to scale the stream up or down, so that you never lose data records prior to their expiration.

Multiple Amazon Kinesis Data Streams applications can consume data from a stream, so that multiple actions, like archiving and processing, can take place concurrently and independently. For example, two applications can read data from the same stream. The first application calculates running aggregates and updates a DynamoDB table, and the second application compresses and archives data to a data store like Amazon S3. The DynamoDB table with running aggregates is then read by a dashboard for up-to-the-minute reports.

The Kinesis Client Library enables fault-tolerant consumption of data from streams and provides scaling support for Amazon Kinesis Data Streams applications.

Related Services

For examples of how to use Amazon EMR clusters to read and process Kinesis data streams directly, see Analyze Kinesis Data Streams Data in the *Amazon EMR Developer Guide*.

Amazon Kinesis Data Streams Key Concepts

As you get started with Amazon Kinesis Data Streams, you'll benefit from understanding its architecture and terminology.

Kinesis Data Streams High-Level Architecture

The following diagram illustrates the high-level architecture of Kinesis Data Streams. The producers continually push data to Kinesis Data Streams and the consumers process the data in real time. Consumers (such as a custom application running on Amazon EC2, or an Amazon Kinesis Data Firehose delivery stream) can store their results using an AWS service such as Amazon DynamoDB, Amazon Redshift, or Amazon S3.

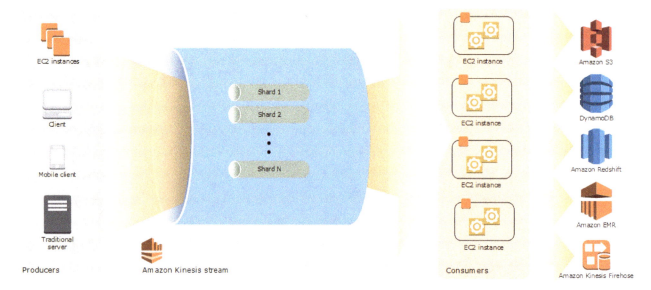

Kinesis Data Streams Terminology

Kinesis Data Streams

A *Kinesis data stream* is a set of shards. Each shard has a sequence of data records. Each data record has a sequence number that is assigned by Kinesis Data Streams.

Data Records

A *data record* is the unit of data stored in a Kinesis data stream. Data records are composed of a sequence number, partition key, and data blob, which is an immutable sequence of bytes. Kinesis Data Streams does not inspect, interpret, or change the data in the blob in any way. A data blob can be up to 1 MB.

Retention Period

The length of time data records are accessible after they are added to the stream. A stream's retention period is set to a default of 24 hours after creation. You can increase the retention period up to 168 hours (7 days) using the IncreaseStreamRetentionPeriod operation, and decrease the retention period down to a minimum of 24 hours using the DecreaseStreamRetentionPeriod operation. Additional charges apply for streams with a retention period set to more than 24 hours. For more information, see Amazon Kinesis Data Streams Pricing.

Producers

Producers put records into Amazon Kinesis Data Streams. For example, a web server sending log data to a stream is a producer.

Consumers

Consumers get records from Amazon Kinesis Data Streams and process them. These consumers are known as Amazon Kinesis Data Streams Applications.

Amazon Kinesis Data Streams Applications

An *Amazon Kinesis Data Streams application* is a consumer of a stream that commonly runs on a fleet of EC2 instances.

You can develop an Amazon Kinesis Data Streams application using the Kinesis Client Library or using the Kinesis Data Streams API.

The output of an Amazon Kinesis Data Streams application may be input for another stream, enabling you to create complex topologies that process data in real time. An application can also send data to a variety of other AWS services. There can be multiple applications for one stream, and each application can consume data from the stream independently and concurrently.

Shards

A *shard* is a uniquely identified sequence of data records in a stream. A stream is composed of one or more shards, each of which provides a fixed unit of capacity. Each shard can support up to 5 transactions per second for reads, up to a maximum total data read rate of 2 MB per second and up to 1,000 records per second for writes, up to a maximum total data write rate of 1 MB per second (including partition keys). The data capacity of your stream is a function of the number of shards that you specify for the stream. The total capacity of the stream is the sum of the capacities of its shards.

If your data rate increases, you can increase or decrease the number of shards allocated to your stream.

Partition Keys

A *partition key* is used to group data by shard within a stream. The Kinesis Data Streams service segregates the data records belonging to a stream into multiple shards, using the partition key associated with each data record to determine which shard a given data record belongs to. Partition keys are Unicode strings with a maximum length limit of 256 bytes. An MD5 hash function is used to map partition keys to 128-bit integer values and to map associated data records to shards. When an application puts data into a stream, it must specfy a partition key.

Sequence Numbers

Each data record has a sequence number that is unique within its shard. The sequence number is assigned by Kinesis Data Streams after you write to the stream with `client.putRecords` or `client.putRecord`. Sequence numbers for the same partition key generally increase over time; the longer the time period between write requests, the larger the sequence numbers become.

Note
Sequence numbers cannot be used as indexes to sets of data within the same stream. To logically separate sets of data, use partition keys or create a separate stream for each dataset.

Kinesis Client Library

The Kinesis Client Library is compiled into your application to enable fault-tolerant consumption of data from the stream. The Kinesis Client Library ensures that for every shard there is a record processor running and processing that shard. The library also simplifies reading data from the stream. The Kinesis Client Library uses an Amazon DynamoDB table to store control data. It creates one table per application that is processing data.

Application Name

The name of an Amazon Kinesis Data Streams application identifies the application. Each of your applications must have a unique name that is scoped to the AWS account and region used by the application. This name is used as a name for the control table in Amazon DynamoDB and the namespace for Amazon CloudWatch metrics.

Server-side encryption

Amazon Kinesis Data Streams can automatically encrypt sensitive data as a producer enters it into a stream. Kinesis Data Streams uses KMS master keys for encryption. For more information, see Using Server-Side Encryption.

Note

To read from or write to an encrypted stream, producer and consumer applications must have permission to access the master key. For information on granting permissions to producer and consumer applications, see Permissions to Use User-Generated KMS Master Keys.

Note

Using server-side encryption incurs KMS costs. For more information, see AWS Key Management Service Pricing.

Kinesis Data Streams

Amazon Kinesis Data Streams ingests a large amount of data in real time, durably stores the data, and makes the data available for consumption. The unit of data stored by Kinesis Data Streams is a *data record*. A *stream* represents a group of data records. The data records in a stream are distributed into shards.

A *shard* has a sequence of data records in a stream. When you create a stream, you specify the number of shards for the stream. Each shard can support up to 5 transactions per second for reads, up to a maximum total data read rate of 2 MB per second. Shards also support up to 1,000 records per second for writes, up to a maximum total data write rate of 1 MB per second (including partition keys). The total capacity of a stream is the sum of the capacities of its shards. You can increase or decrease the number of shards in a stream as needed. However, you are charged on a per-shard basis.

A producer puts data records into shards and a consumer gets data records from shards.

Determining the Initial Size of a Kinesis Data Stream

Before you create a stream, you need to determine an initial size for the stream. After you create the stream, you can dynamically scale your shard capacity up or down using the AWS Management Console or the UpdateShardCount API. You can make updates while there is an Amazon Kinesis Data Streams application consuming data from the stream.

To determine the initial size of a stream, you need the following input values:

- The average size of the data record written to the stream in kilobytes (KB), rounded up to the nearest 1 KB, the data size (`average_data_size_in_KB`).
- The number of data records written to and read from the stream per second (`records_per_second`).
- The number of Amazon Kinesis Data Streams applications that consume data concurrently and independently from the stream, that is, the consumers (`number_of_consumers`).
- The incoming write bandwidth in KB (`incoming_write_bandwidth_in_KB`), which is equal to the `average_data_size_in_KB` multiplied by the `records_per_second`.
- The outgoing read bandwidth in KB (`outgoing_read_bandwidth_in_KB`), which is equal to the `incoming_write_bandwidth_in_KB` multiplied by the `number_of_consumers`.

You can calculate the initial number of shards (`number_of_shards`) that your stream will need by using the input values in the following formula:

```
1  number_of_shards = max(incoming_write_bandwidth_in_KB/1000, outgoing_read_bandwidth_in_KB/2000)
```

Creating a Stream

You can create a stream using the Kinesis Data Streams console, the Kinesis Data Streams API, or the AWS CLI.

To create a stream using the console

1. Open the Kinesis Data Streams console at https://console.aws.amazon.com/kinesis/.

2. In the navigation bar, expand the region selector and choose a region.

3. Choose **Create Stream**.

4. On the **Create Stream** page, enter a name for your stream and the number of shards you need, and then click **Create**.

   On the **Stream List** page, your stream's **Status** is CREATING while the stream is being created. When the stream is ready to use, the **Status** changes to ACTIVE.

5. Choose the name of your stream. The **Stream Details** page displays a summary of your stream configuration, along with monitoring information.

To create a stream using the Kinesis Data Streams API

- For information about creating a stream using the Kinesis Data Streams API, see Creating a Stream.

To create a stream using the AWS CLI

- For information about creating a stream using the AWS CLI, see the create-stream command.

Updating a Stream

You can update the details of a stream using the Kinesis Data Streams console, the Kinesis Data Streams API, or the AWS CLI.

Note
You can enable server-side encryption for existing streams, or for streams that you have recently created.

To update a stream using the console

1. Open the Kinesis Data Streams console at https://console.aws.amazon.com/kinesis/.

2. In the navigation bar, expand the region selector and select a region.

3. Choose the name of your stream. The **Stream Details** page displays a summary of your stream configuration and monitoring information.

4. To edit the number of shards, choose **Edit** in the **Shards** section, and then enter a new shard count.

5. To enable server-side encryption of data records, choose **Edit** in the **Server-side encryption** section. Choose a KMS key to use as the master key for encryption, or use the default master key, **aws/kinesis**, managed by Kinesis. If you enable encryption for a stream and use your own KMS master key, ensure that your producer and consumer applications have access to the KMS master key you used. To assign permissions to an application to access a user-generated KMS key, see Permissions to Use User-Generated KMS Master Keys

6. To edit the data retention period, choose **Edit** in the **Data retention period** section, and then enter a new data retention period.

7. If you have enabled custom metrics on your account, choose **Edit** in the **Shard level metrics** section, and then specify metrics for your stream. For more information, see Monitoring the Amazon Kinesis Data Streams Service with Amazon CloudWatch.

Updating a Stream Using the API

To update stream details using the API, see the following methods:
- AddTagsToStream
- DecreaseStreamRetentionPeriod
- DisableEnhancedMonitoring
- EnableEnhancedMonitoring
- IncreaseStreamRetentionPeriod
- RemoveTagsFromStream
- StartStreamEncryption
- StopStreamEncryption
- UpdateShardCount

Updating a Stream Using the CLI

For information about updating a stream using the AWS CLI, see the Kinesis CLI reference.

Producers for Amazon Kinesis Data Streams

A *producer* puts data records into Kinesis data streams. For example, a web server sending log data to a Kinesis data stream is a producer. A consumer processes the data records from a stream.

Important
Changing the Data Retention Period

To put data into the stream, you must specify the name of the stream, a partition key, and the data blob to be added to the stream. The partition key is used to determine which shard in the stream the data record is added to.

All the data in the shard is sent to the same worker that is processing the shard. Which partition key you use depends on your application logic. The number of partition keys should typically be much greater than the number of shards. This is because the partition key is used to determine how to map a data record to a particular shard. If you have enough partition keys, the data can be evenly distributed across the shards in a stream.

For more information, see Adding Data to a Stream (includes Java example code), the PutRecords and PutRecord operations in the Kinesis Data Streams API, or the put-record command.

Consumers for Amazon Kinesis Data Streams

A consumer gets data records from Kinesis data streams. A consumer, known as a *Amazon Kinesis Data Streams application*, processes the data records from a stream.

Important
Changing the Data Retention Period

Note
To save stream records directly to storage services such as Amazon S3, Amazon Redshift, or Amazon Elasticsearch Service, you can use a Kinesis Data Firehose delivery stream instead of creating a consumer application. For more information, see Creating an Amazon Kinesis Firehose Delivery Stream.

Each consumer reads from a particular shard, using a shard iterator. A *shard iterator* represents the position in the stream from which the consumer reads. When they start reading from a stream, consumers get a shard iterator, which can be used to change where the consumers read from the stream. When the consumer performs a read operation, it receives a batch of data records based on the position specified by the shard iterator.

Each consumer must have a unique name that is scoped to the AWS account and region used by the application. This name is used as a name for the control table in Amazon DynamoDB and the namespace for Amazon CloudWatch metrics. When your application starts up, it creates an Amazon DynamoDB table to store the application state, connects to the specified stream, and then starts consuming data from the stream. You can view the Kinesis Data Streams metrics using the CloudWatch console.

You can deploy the consumer to an EC2 instance by adding to one of your AMIs. You can scale the consumer by running it on multiple EC2 instances under an Auto Scaling group. Using an Auto Scaling group helps automatically start new instances in the event of an EC2 instance failure and can also elastically scale the number of instances as the load on the application changes over time. Auto Scaling groups ensure that a certain number of EC2 instances are always running. To trigger scaling events in the Auto Scaling group, you can specify metrics such as CPU and memory utilization to scale up or down the number of EC2 instances processing data from the stream. For more information, see the Amazon EC2 Auto Scaling User Guide.

You can use the Kinesis Client Library (KCL) to simplify parallel processing of the stream by a fleet of workers running on a fleet of EC2 instances. The KCL simplifies writing code to read from the shards in the stream and ensures that there is a worker allocated to every shard in the stream. The KCL also provides help with fault tolerance by providing checkpointing capabilities. The best way to get started with the KCL is to review the samples in Developing Amazon Kinesis Data Streams Consumers Using the Kinesis Client Library.

Amazon Kinesis Data Streams Limits

Kinesis Data Streams has following limits.

- The default shard limit is 500 shards for the following regions: US East (N. Virginia), US West (Oregon), and EU (Ireland). For all other regions, the default shard limit is 200 shards. There is no upper limit to the number of shards in a stream or account. To view your limits and the number of shards in use, use the DescribeLimits API or the describe-limits command. To request an increase in your shard limit, use the Kinesis Data Streams Limits form.
- Changing the Data Retention Period
- The maximum size of a data blob (the data payload before base64-encoding) is up to 1 MB.
- AddTagsToStream, ListTagsForStream, and RemoveTagsFromStream can provide up to 5 transactions per second per account.
- CreateStream, DeleteStream, and ListStreams can provide up to 5 transactions per second.
- DescribeStream can provide up to 10 transactions per second.
- DescribeStreamSummary can provide up to 20 transactions per second.
- GetRecords can retrieve 10 MB of data.
- DescribeLimits can provide up to 1 transaction per second.
- GetShardIterator can provide up to 5 transactions per second per open shard.
- ListShards has a limit of 100 transactions per second per data stream.
- MergeShards and SplitShard can provide up to 5 transactions per second.
- UpdateShardCount provides up to 2 calls per rolling 24-hour period per stream. By default, the API can scale up to either your shard limit or 500 shards, whichever is lower. To request an increase in the call rate limit, the shard limit for this API, or your overall shard limit, use the Kinesis Data Streams Limits form.
- Each shard can support up to 5 transactions per second for reads, up to a maximum total data read rate of 2 MB per second.
- Each shard can support up to 1,000 records per second for writes, up to a maximum total data write rate of 1 MB per second (including partition keys). This write limit applies to operations such as PutRecord and PutRecords.
- A shard iterator returned by GetShardIterator times out after 5 minutes if you haven't used it.

Read limits are based on the number of open shards. For more information about shard states, see Data Routing, Data Persistence, and Shard State after a Reshard.

Many of these limits are directly related to API operations. For more information, see the Amazon Kinesis API Reference.

Getting Started Using Amazon Kinesis Data Streams

This documentation helps you get started using Amazon Kinesis Data Streams. If you are new to Kinesis Data Streams, start by becoming familiar with the concepts and terminology presented in What Is Amazon Kinesis Data Streams?.

Topics

- Setting Up for Amazon Kinesis Data Streams
- Tutorial: Visualizing Web Traffic Using Amazon Kinesis Data Streams
- Tutorial: Getting Started With Amazon Kinesis Data Streams Using AWS CLI

Setting Up for Amazon Kinesis Data Streams

Before you use Amazon Kinesis Data Streams for the first time, complete the following tasks.

Topics
- Sign Up for AWS
- Download Libraries and Tools
- Configure Your Development Environment

Sign Up for AWS

When you sign up for Amazon Web Services (AWS), your AWS account is automatically signed up for all services in AWS, including Kinesis Data Streams. You are charged only for the services that you use.

If you have an AWS account already, skip to the next task. If you don't have an AWS account, use the following procedure to create one.

To sign up for an AWS account

1. Open https://aws.amazon.com/, and then choose **Create an AWS Account**. **Note**
   This might be unavailable in your browser if you previously signed into the AWS Management Console. In that case, choose **Sign in to a different account**, and then choose **Create a new AWS account**.

2. Follow the online instructions.

   Part of the sign-up procedure involves receiving a phone call and entering a PIN using the phone keypad.

Download Libraries and Tools

The following libraries and tools will help you work with Kinesis Data Streams:

- The Amazon Kinesis API Reference is the basic set of operations that Kinesis Data Streams supports. For more information about performing basic operations using Java code, see the following:
  - Developing Amazon Kinesis Data Streams Producers Using the Amazon Kinesis Data Streams API with the AWS SDK for Java
  - Developing Amazon Kinesis Data Streams Consumers Using the Amazon Kinesis Data Streams API with the AWS SDK for Java
  - Managing Kinesis Data Streams Using Java
- The AWS SDKs for Java, JavaScript, .NET, Node.js, PHP, Python, and Ruby include Kinesis Data Streams support and samples. If your version of the AWS SDK for Java does not include samples for Kinesis Data Streams, you can also download them from GitHub.
- The Kinesis Client Library (KCL) provides an easy-to-use programming model for processing data. The KCL can help you get started quickly with Kinesis Data Streams in Java, Node.js, .NET, Python, and Ruby. For more information see Developing Amazon Kinesis Data Streams Consumers Using the Kinesis Client Library.
- The AWS Command Line Interface supports Kinesis Data Streams. The AWS CLI enables you to control multiple AWS services from the command line and automate them through scripts.
- (Optional) The Kinesis Connector Library helps you integrate Kinesis Data Streams with other AWS services. For example, you can use the Kinesis Connector Library, in conjunction with the KCL, to reliably move data from Kinesis Data Streams to Amazon DynamoDB, Amazon Redshift, and Amazon S3.

Configure Your Development Environment

To use the KCL, ensure that your Java development environment meets the following requirements:

- Java 1.7 (Java SE 7 JDK) or later. You can download the latest Java software from Java SE Downloads on the Oracle website.
- Apache Commons package (Code, HTTP Client, and Logging)
- Jackson JSON processor

Note that the AWS SDK for Java includes Apache Commons and Jackson in the third-party folder. However, the SDK for Java works with Java 1.6, while the Kinesis Client Library requires Java 1.7.

Tutorial: Visualizing Web Traffic Using Amazon Kinesis Data Streams

This tutorial helps you get started using Amazon Kinesis Data Streams by providing an introduction to key Kinesis Data Streams constructs; specifically streams, data producers, and data consumers. The tutorial uses a sample application based upon a common use case of real-time data analytics, as introduced in What Is Amazon Kinesis Data Streams?.

The web application for this sample uses a simple JavaScript application to poll the DynamoDB table used to store the results of the Top-N analysis over a slide window. The application takes this data and creates a visualization of the results.

Kinesis Data Streams Data Visualization Sample Application

The data visualization sample application for this tutorial demonstrates how to use Kinesis Data Streams for real-time data ingestion and analysis. The sample application creates a data producer that puts simulated visitor counts from various URLs into a Kinesis data stream. The stream durably stores these data records in the order they are received. The data consumer gets these records from the stream, and then calculates how many visitors originated from a particular URL. Finally, a simple web application polls the results in real time to provide a visualization of the calculations.

The sample application demonstrates the common stream processing use-case of performing a sliding window analysis over a 10-second period. The data displayed in the above visualization reflects the results of the sliding window analysis of the stream as a continuously updated graph. In addition, the data consumer performs Top-K analysis over the data stream to compute the top three referrers by count, which is displayed in the table immediately below the graph and updated every two seconds.

To get you started quickly, the sample application uses AWS CloudFormation. AWS CloudFormation allows you to create templates to describe the AWS resources and any associated dependencies or runtime parameters required to run your application. The sample application uses a template to create all the necessary resources quickly, including producer and consumer applications running on an Amazon EC2 instance and a table in Amazon DynamoDB to store the aggregate record counts.

Note
After the sample application starts, it incurs nominal charges for Kinesis Data Streams usage. Where possible, the sample application uses resources that are eligible for the AWS Free Tier. When you are finished with this tutorial, delete your AWS resources to stop incurring charges. For more information, see Step 3: Delete Sample Application.

Prerequisites

This tutorial helps you set up, run, and view the results of the Kinesis Data Streams data visualization sample application. To get started with the sample application, you first need to do the following:

- Set up a computer with a working Internet connection.
- Sign up for an AWS account.
- Additionally, read through the introductory sections to gain a high-level understanding of streams, data producers, and data consumers.

Step 1: Start the Sample Application

Start the sample application using a AWS CloudFormation template provided by AWS. The sample application has a stream writer that randomly generates records and sends them to an Kinesis data stream, a data consumer that counts the number of HTTPS requests to a resource, and a web application that displays the outputs of the stream processing data as a continuously updated graph.

To start the application

1. Open the AWS CloudFormation template for this tutorial.

2. On the **Select Template** page, the URL for the template is provided. Choose **Next**.

3. On the **Specify Details** page, note that the default instance type is `t2.micro`. However, T2 instances require a VPC. If your AWS account does not have a default VPC in your region, you must change **InstanceType** another instance type, such as `m3.medium`. Choose **Next**.

4. On the **Options** page, you can optionally type a tag key and tag value. This tag will be added to the resources created by the template, such as the EC2 instance. Choose **Next**.

5. On the **Review page**, select **I acknowledge that this template might cause AWS CloudFormation to create IAM resources**, and then choose **Create**.

Initially, you should see a stack named **KinesisDataVisSample** with the status `CREATE_IN_PROGRESS`. The stack can take several minutes to create. When the status is `CREATE_COMPLETE`, continue to the next step. If the status does not update, refresh the page.

Step 2: View the Components of the Sample Application

Topics
- Kinesis Data Stream
- Data Producer
- Data Consumer

Kinesis Data Stream

A stream has the ability to ingest data in real-time from a large number of producers, durably store the data, and provide the data to multiple consumers. A stream represents an ordered sequence of data records. When you create a stream, you must specify a stream name and a shard count. A stream consists of one or more shards; each shard is a group of data records.

AWS CloudFormation automatically creates the stream for the sample application. This section of the AWS CloudFormation template shows the parameters used in the CreateStream operation.

To view the stack details

1. Select the **KinesisDataVisSample** stack.

2. On the **Outputs** tab, choose the link in **URL**. The form of the URL should be similar to the following: http://ec2/-xx/-xx/-xx/-xx/.compute/-1/.amazonaws/.com/.

3. It takes about 10 minutes for the application stack to be created and for meaningful data to show up in the data analysis graph. The real-time data analysis graph appears on a separate page, titled **Kinesis Data Streams Data Visualization Sample**. It displays the number of requests sent by the referring URL over a 10 second span, and the chart is updated every 1 second. The span of the graph is the last 2 minutes.

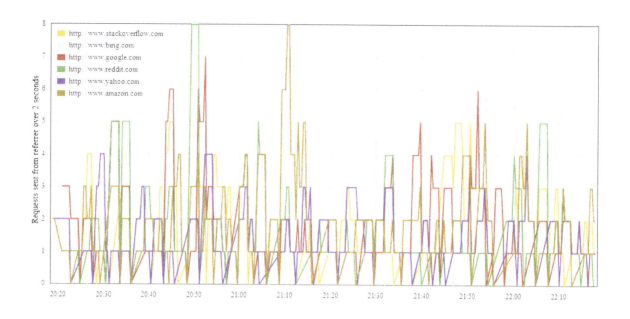

Top 3 referrers by counts (Updated every 2000ms):

http://www.amazon.com	489
http://www.google.com	461
http://www.stackoverflow.com	455

To view the stream details

1. Open the Kinesis console at https://console.aws.amazon.com/kinesis.

2. Select the stream whose name has the following form: `KinesisDataVisSampleApp-KinesisStream-[randomString]`.

3. Choose the name of the stream to view the stream details.

4. The graphs display the activity of the data producer putting records into the stream and the data consumer getting data from the stream.

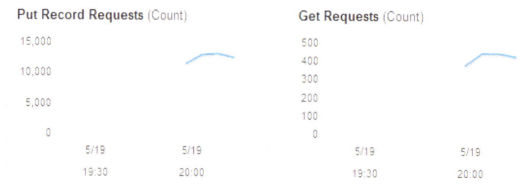

Data Producer

A data producer submits data records to the Kinesis data stream. To put data into the stream, producers call the PutRecord operation on a stream.

Each `PutRecord` call requires the stream name, partition key, and the data record that the producer is adding to the stream. The stream name determines the stream in which the record will reside. The partition key is used to determine the shard in the stream that the data record will be added to.

Which partition key you use depends on your application logic. The number of partition keys should be much greater than the number of shards. in most cases. A high number of partition keys relative to shards allows the stream to distribute data records evenly across the shards in your stream.

The data producer uses six popular URLs as a partition key for each record put into the two-shard stream. These URLs represent simulated page visits. Rows 99-132 of the HttpReferrerKinesisPutter code send the data to Kinesis Data Streams. The three required parameters are set before calling `PutRecord`. The partition key is set using `pair.getResource`, which randomly selects one of the six URLs created in rows 85-92 of the HttpReferrerStreamWriter code.

A data producer can be anything that puts data to Kinesis Data Streams, such as an EC2 instance, client browser, or mobile device. The sample application uses an EC2 instance for its data producer as well as its data consumer; whereas, most real-life scenarios would have separate EC2 instances for each component of the application. You can view EC2 instance data from the sample application by following the instructions below.

To view the instance data in the console

1. Open the Amazon EC2 console at https://console.aws.amazon.com/ec2/.

2. On the navigation pane, choose **Instances**.

3. Select the instance created for the sample application. If you aren't sure which instance this is, it has a security group with a name that starts with **KinesisDataVisSample**.

4. On the **Monitoring** tab, you'll see the resource usage of the sample application's data producer and data consumer.

Data Consumer

Data consumers retrieve and process data records from shards in a Kinesis data stream. Each consumer reads data from a particular shard. Consumers retrieve data from a shard using the GetShardIterator and GetRecords operations.

A shard iterator represents the position of the stream and shard from which the consumer will read. A consumer gets a shard iterator when it starts reading from a stream or changes the position from which it reads records from a stream. To get a shard iterator, you must provide a stream name, shard ID, and shard iterator type. The shard iterator type allows the consumer to specify where in the stream it would like to start reading from, such as from the start of the stream where the data is arriving in real-time. The stream returns the records in a batch, whose size you can control using the optional limit parameter.

The data consumer creates a table in DynamoDB to maintain state information (such as checkpoints and worker-shard mapping) for the application. Each application has its own DynamoDB table.

The data consumer counts visitor requests from each particular URL over the last two seconds. This type of real-time application employs Top-N analysis over a sliding window. In this case, the Top-N are the top three pages by visitor requests and the sliding window is two seconds. This is a common processing pattern that is demonstrative of real-world data analyses using Kinesis Data Streams. The results of this calculation are persisted to a DynamoDB table.

To view the Amazon DynamoDB tables

1. Open the DynamoDB console at https://console.aws.amazon.com/dynamodb/.

2. On the navigation pane, select **Tables**.

3. There are two tables created by the sample application:

   - KinesisDataVisSampleApp-KCLDynamoDBTable-[randomString]—Manages state information.

- KinesisDataVisSampleApp-CountsDynamoDBTable-[randomString]—Persists the results of the Top-N analysis over a sliding window.

4. Select the KinesisDataVisSampleApp-KCLDynamoDBTable-[randomString] table. There are two entries in the table, indicating the particular shard (leaseKey), position in the stream (checkpoint), and the application reading the data (leaseOwner).

5. Select the KinesisDataVisSampleApp-CountsDynamoDBTable-[randomString] table. You can see the aggregated visitor counts (referrerCounts) that the data consumer calculates as part of the sliding window analysis.

Kinesis Client Library (KCL)

Consumer applications can use the Kinesis Client Library (KCL) to simplify parallel processing of the stream. The KCL takes care of many of the complex tasks associated with distributed computing, such as load-balancing across multiple instances, responding to instance failures, checkpointing processed records, and reacting to resharding. The KCL enables you to focus on writing record processing logic.

The data consumer provides the KCL with position of the stream that it wants to read from, in this case specifying the latest possible data from the beginning of the stream. The library uses this to call `GetShardIterator` on behalf of the consumer. The consumer component also provides the client library with what to do with the records that are processed using an important KCL interface called `IRecordProcessor`. The KCL calls `GetRecords` on behalf of the consumer and then processes those records as specified by `IRecordProcessor`.

- Rows 92-98 of the HttpReferrerCounterApplication sample code configure the KCL. This sets up the library with its initial configuration, such as the setting the position of the stream in which to read data.
- Rows 104-108 of the HttpReferrerCounterApplication sample code inform the KCL of what logic to use when processing records using an important client library component, `IRecordProcessor`.
- Rows 186-203 of the CountingRecordProcessor sample code include the counting logic for the Top-N analysis using `IRecordProcessor`.

Step 3: Delete Sample Application

The sample application creates two shards, which incur shard usage charges while the application runs. To ensure that your AWS account does not continue to be billed, delete your AWS CloudFormation stack after you finish with the sample application.

To delete application resources

1. Open the AWS CloudFormation console at https://console.aws.amazon.com/cloudformation.

2. Select the stack.

3. Choose **Actions**, **Delete Stack**

4. When prompted for confirmation, choose **Yes, Delete**.

The status changes to `DELETE_IN_PROGRESS` while AWS CloudFormation cleans up the resources associated with the sample application. When AWS CloudFormation is finished cleaning up the resources, it removes the stack from the list.

Step 4: Next Steps

- You can explore the source code for the Data Visualization Sample Application on GitHub.
- You can find more advanced material about using the Kinesis Data Streams API in the Developing Amazon Kinesis Data Streams Producers Using the Amazon Kinesis Data Streams API with the AWS SDK for Java, Developing Amazon Kinesis Data Streams Consumers Using the Amazon Kinesis Data Streams API with the AWS SDK for Java, and Managing Kinesis Data Streams Using Java.

- You can find sample application in the AWS SDK for Java that uses the SDK to put and get data from Kinesis Data Streams.

Tutorial: Getting Started With Amazon Kinesis Data Streams Using AWS CLI

This tutorial shows you how to perform basic Amazon Kinesis Data Streams operations using the AWS Command Line Interface. You will learn fundamental Kinesis Data Streams data flow principles and the steps necessary to put and get data from an Kinesis data stream.

For CLI access, you need an access key ID and secret access key. Use IAM user access keys instead of AWS account root user access keys. IAM lets you securely control access to AWS services and resources in your AWS account. For more information about creating access keys, see Understanding and Getting Your Security Credentials in the *AWS General Reference*.

You can find detailed step-by-step IAM and security key set up instructions at Create an IAM User.

In this tutorial, the specific commands discussed will be given verbatim, except where specific values will necessarily be different for each run. Also, the examples are using the US West (Oregon) region, but this tutorial will work on any of the regions that support Kinesis Data Streams.

Topics

- Install and Configure the AWS CLI
- Perform Basic Stream Operations

Install and Configure the AWS CLI

Install AWS CLI

Use the following process to install the AWS CLI for Windows and for Linux, OS X, and Unix operating systems.

Windows

1. Download the appropriate MSI installer from the Windows section of the full installation instructions in the AWS Command Line Interface User Guide.

2. Run the downloaded MSI installer.

3. Follow the instructions that appear.

Linux, macOS, or Unix

These steps require Python 2.6.5 or higher. If you have any problems, see the full installation instructions in the AWS Command Line Interface User Guide.

1. Download and run the installation script from the pip website:

```
1 curl "https://bootstrap.pypa.io/get-pip.py" -o "get-pip.py"
2 sudo python get-pip.py
```

2. Install the AWS CLI Using Pip.

```
1 sudo pip install awscli
```

Use the following command to list available options and services:

```
1 aws help
```

You will be using the Kinesis Data Streams service, so you can review the AWS CLI subcommands related to Kinesis Data Streams using the following command:

```
1 aws kinesis help
```

This command results in output that includes the available Kinesis Data Streams commands:

```
 1 AVAILABLE COMMANDS
 2
 3       o add-tags-to-stream
 4
 5       o create-stream
 6
 7       o delete-stream
 8
 9       o describe-stream
10
11       o get-records
12
13       o get-shard-iterator
14
15       o help
16
```

```
17      o list-streams
18
19      o list-tags-for-stream
20
21      o merge-shards
22
23      o put-record
24
25      o put-records
26
27      o remove-tags-from-stream
28
29      o split-shard
30
31      o wait
```

This command list corresponds to the Kinesis Data Streams API documented in the Amazon Kinesis Service API Reference. For example, the `create-stream` command corresponds to the `CreateStream` API action.

The AWS CLI is now successfully installed, but not configured. This is shown in the next section.

Configure AWS CLI

For general use, the `aws configure` command is the fastest way to set up your AWS CLI installation. This is a one-time setup if your preferences don't change because the AWS CLI remembers your settings between sessions.

```
1 aws configure
2 AWS Access Key ID [None]: AKIAIOSFODNN7EXAMPLE
3 AWS Secret Access Key [None]: wJalrXUtnFEMI/K7MDENG/bPxRfiCYEXAMPLEKEY
4 Default region name [None]: us-west-2
5 Default output format [None]: json
```

The AWS CLI will prompt you for four pieces of information. The AWS access key ID and the AWS secret access key are your account credentials. If you don't have keys, see Sign Up for Amazon Web Services.

The default region is the name of the region you want to make calls against by default. This is usually the region closest to you, but it can be any region.

Note
You must specify an AWS region when using the AWS CLI. For a list of services and available regions, see Regions and Endpoints.

The default output format can be either JSON, text, or table. If you don't specify an output format, JSON will be used.

For more information about the files that `aws configure` creates, additional settings, and named profiles, see Configuring the AWS Command Line Interface in the AWS Command Line Interface User Guide.

Perform Basic Stream Operations

This section describes basic use of an Kinesis data stream from the command line using the AWS CLI. Be sure you are familiar with the concepts discussed in Amazon Kinesis Data Streams Key Concepts and Tutorial: Visualizing Web Traffic Using Amazon Kinesis Data Streams.

Note
After you create a stream, your account incurs nominal charges for Kinesis Data Streams usage because Kinesis Data Streams is not eligible for the AWS free tier. When you are finished with this tutorial, delete your AWS resources to stop incurring charges. For more information, see Step 4: Clean Up.

Topics
- Step 1: Create a Stream
- Step 2: Put a Record
- Step 3: Get the Record
- Step 4: Clean Up

Step 1: Create a Stream

Your first step is to create a stream and verify that it was successfully created. Use the following command to create a stream named "Foo":

```
1 aws kinesis create-stream --stream-name Foo --shard-count 1
```

The parameter `--shard-count` is required, and for this part of the tutorial you are using one shard in your stream. Next, issue the following command to check on the stream's creation progress:

```
1 aws kinesis describe-stream --stream-name Foo
```

You should get output that is similar to the following example:

```
1 {
2     "StreamDescription": {
3         "StreamStatus": "CREATING",
4         "StreamName": "Foo",
5         "StreamARN": "arn:aws:kinesis:us-west-2:account-id:stream/Foo",
6         "Shards": []
7     }
8 }
```

In this example, the stream has a status CREATING, which means it is not quite ready to use. Check again in a few moments, and you should see output similar to the following example:

```
1 {
2     "StreamDescription": {
3         "StreamStatus": "ACTIVE",
4         "StreamName": "Foo",
5         "StreamARN": "arn:aws:kinesis:us-west-2:account-id:stream/Foo",
6         "Shards": [
7             {
8                 "ShardId": "shardId-000000000000",
9                 "HashKeyRange": {
10                     "EndingHashKey": "170141183460469231731687303715884105727",
11                     "StartingHashKey": "0"
12                 },
13                 "SequenceNumberRange": {
```

```
14                      "StartingSequenceNumber":
                            "49546986683135544286507457935754639466300920667981217794"
15                  }
16              }
17          ]
18      }
19 }
```

There is information in this output that you don't need to be concerned about for this tutorial. The main thing for now is `"StreamStatus": "ACTIVE"`, which tells you that the stream is ready to be used, and the information on the single shard that you requested. You can also verify the existence of your new stream by using the `list-streams` command, as shown here:

```
1 aws kinesis list-streams
```

Output:

```
1 {
2     "StreamNames": [
3         "Foo"
4     ]
5 }
```

Step 2: Put a Record

Now that you have an active stream, you are ready to put some data. For this tutorial, you will use the simplest possible command, `put-record`, which puts a single data record containing the text "testdata" into the stream:

```
1 aws kinesis put-record --stream-name Foo --partition-key 123 --data testdata
```

This command, if successful, will result in output similar to the following example:

```
1 {
2     "ShardId": "shardId-000000000000",
3     "SequenceNumber": "49546986683135544286507457936321625675700192471156785154"
4 }
```

Congratulations, you just added data to a stream! Next you will see how to get data out of the stream.

Step 3: Get the Record

Before you can get data from the stream you need to obtain the shard iterator for the shard you are interested in. A shard iterator represents the position of the stream and shard from which the consumer (`get-record` command in this case) will read. You'll use the `get-shard-iterator` command, as follows:

```
1 aws kinesis get-shard-iterator --shard-id shardId-000000000000 --shard-iterator-type
     TRIM_HORIZON --stream-name Foo
```

Recall that the `aws kinesis` commands have a Kinesis Data Streams API behind them, so if you are curious about any of the parameters shown, you can read about them in the http://docs.aws.amazon.com/kinesis/latest/APIReference/API_GetShardIterator.html API reference topic. Successful execution will result in output similar to the following example (scroll horizontally to see the entire output):

```
1 {
2     "ShardIterator": "AAAAAAAAAAHSywljvOzEgPX4NyKdZ5wryMzP9yALs8NeKbUjp1IxtZs1Sp+
           KEd9I6AJ9ZG41NR1EMi+9Md/nHvtLyxpfhEzYvkTZ4D9DQVz/mBYWRO6OTZRKnW9gd+
           efGN2aHFdkH1rJl4BL9Wyrk+ghYG22D2T1Da2EyNSH1+LAbK33gQweTJADBdyMwlo5r6PqcP2dzhg="
3 }
```

The long string of seemingly random characters is the shard iterator (yours will be different). You will need to copy/paste the shard iterator into the get command, shown next. Shard iterators have a valid lifetime of 300 seconds, which should be enough time for you to copy/paste the shard iterator into the next command. Notice you will need to remove any newlines from your shard iterator before pasting to the next command. If you get an error message that the shard iterator is no longer valid, simply execute the `get-shard-iterator` command again.

The `get-records` command gets data from the stream, and it resolves to a call to http://docs.aws.amazon.com/kinesis/latest/APIReference/API_GetRecords.html in the Kinesis Data Streams API. The shard iterator specifies the position in the shard from which you want to start reading data records sequentially. If there are no records available in the portion of the shard that the iterator points to, `GetRecords` returns an empty list. Note that it might take multiple calls to get to a portion of the shard that contains records.

In the following example of the `get-records` command (scroll horizontally to see the entire command):

```
1 aws kinesis get-records --shard-iterator
     AAAAAAAAAAHSywljvOzEgPX4NyKdZ5wryMzP9yALs8NeKbUjp1IxtZs1Sp+KEd9I6AJ9ZG41NR1EMi+9Md/
     nHvtLyxpfhEzYvkTZ4D9DQVz/mBYWRO6OTZRKnW9gd+efGN2aHFdkH1rJl4BL9Wyrk+ghYG22D2T1Da2EyNSH1+
     LAbK33gQweTJADBdyMwlo5r6PqcP2dzhg=
```

If you are running this tutorial from a Unix-type command processor such as bash, you can automate the acquisition of the shard iterator using a nested command, like this (scroll horizontally to see the entire command):

```
1 SHARD_ITERATOR=$(aws kinesis get-shard-iterator --shard-id shardId-000000000000 --shard-iterator
     -type TRIM_HORIZON --stream-name Foo --query 'ShardIterator')
2
3 aws kinesis get-records --shard-iterator $SHARD_ITERATOR
```

If you are running this tutorial from a system that supports PowerShell, you can automate acquisition of the shard iterator using a command such as this (scroll horizontally to see the entire command):

```
1 aws kinesis get-records --shard-iterator ((aws kinesis get-shard-iterator --shard-id shardId
     -000000000000 --shard-iterator-type TRIM_HORIZON --stream-name Foo).split('"')[4])
```

The successful result of the `get-records` command will request records from your stream for the shard that you specified when you obtained the shard iterator, as in the following example (scroll horizontally to see the entire output):

```
1 {
2   "Records":[ {
3     "Data":"dGVzdGRhdGE=",
4     "PartitionKey"":"123,
5     "ApproximateArrivalTimestamp": 1.441215410867E9,
6     "SequenceNumber":"49544985256907370027570885864065577703022652638596431874"
7   } ],
8   "MillisBehindLatest":24000,
9   "NextShardIterator":"AAAAAAAAAAEDOW3ugseWPE4503kqN1yN1UaodY8unE0sYslMUmC61X9hlig5+t4RtZM0/
        tALfiI4QGjunVgJvQsjxjh2aLyxaAaPr+
        LaoENQ7eVs4EdYXgKyThTZGPcca2fVXYJWL3yafv9dsDwsYVedI66dbMZFC8rPMWc797zxQkv4pSKvPOZvrUIudb8UkH3VM
        ="
10 }
```

Note that `get-records` is described above as a *request*, which means you may receive zero or more records even if there are records in your stream, and any records returned may not represent all the records currently in your stream. This is perfectly normal, and production code will simply poll the stream for records at appropriate intervals (this polling speed will vary depending on your specific application design requirements).

The first thing you'll likely notice about your record in this part of the tutorial is that the data appears to be garbage –; it's not the clear text `testdata` we sent. This is due to the way `put-record` uses Base64 encoding to allow you to send binary data. However, the Kinesis Data Streams support in the AWS CLI does not provide Base64 *decoding* because Base64 decoding to raw binary content printed to stdout can lead to undesired behavior and potential security issues on certain platforms and terminals. If you use a Base64 decoder (for example, https://www.base64decode.org/) to manually decode `dGVzdGRhdGE=` you will see that it is, in fact, `testdata`. This is sufficient for the sake of this tutorial because, in practice, the AWS CLI is rarely used to consume data, but more often to monitor the state of the stream and obtain information, as shown previously (`describe-stream` and `list-streams`). Future tutorials will show you how to build production-quality consumer applications using the Kinesis Client Library (KCL), where Base64 is taken care of for you. For more information about the KCL, see Developing Amazon Kinesis Data Streams Consumers Using the Kinesis Client Library.

It's not always the case that `get-records` will return all records in the stream/shard specified. When that happens, use the `NextShardIterator` from the last result to get the next set of records. So if more data were being put into the stream (the normal situation in production applications), you could keep polling for data using `get-records` each time. However, if you do not call `get-records` using the next shard iterator within the 300 second shard iterator lifetime, you will get an error message, and you will need to use the `get-shard-iterator` command to get a fresh shard iterator.

Also provided in this output is `MillisBehindLatest`, which is the number of milliseconds the GetRecords operation's response is from the tip of the stream, indicating how far behind current time the consumer is. A value of zero indicates record processing is caught up, and there are no new records to process at this moment. In the case of this tutorial, you may see a number that's quite large if you've been taking time to read along as you go. That's not a problem, data records will stay in a stream for 24 hours waiting for you to retrieve them. This time frame is called the retention period and it is configurable up to 168 hours (7 days).

Note that a successful `get-records` result will always have a `NextShardIterator` even if there are no more records currently in the stream. This is a polling model that assumes a producer is potentially putting more records into the stream at any given time. Although you can write your own polling routines, if you use the previously mentioned KCL for developing consumer applications, this polling is taken care of for you.

If you call `get-records` until there are no more records in the stream and shard you are pulling from, you will see output with empty records similar to the following example (scroll horizontally to see the entire output):

```
1 {
2     "Records": [],
3     "NextShardIterator": "AAAAAAAAAAAGCJ5jzQNjmdhO6B/YDIDE56jmZmrmMA/r1WjoHXC/
         kPJXc1rckt3TFL55dENfe5meNgdkyCRpUPGzJpMgYHaJ53C3nCAjQ6s7ZupjXeJGoUFs5oCuFwhP+Wul/
         EhyNeSs5DYXLSSC5XCapmCAYGFjYER69QSdQjxMmBPE/hiybFDi5qtkT6/PsZNz6kFoqtDk="
4 }
```

Step 4: Clean Up

Finally, you'll want to delete your stream to free up resources and avoid unintended charges to your account, as previously noted. Do this in practice any time you have created a stream and will not be using it because charges accrue per stream whether you are putting and getting data with it or not. The clean-up command is simple:

```
1 aws kinesis delete-stream --stream-name Foo
```

Success results in no output, so you might want to use `describe-stream` to check on deletion progress:

```
1 aws kinesis describe-stream --stream-name Foo
```

If you execute this command immediately after the delete command, you will likely see output similar to the following example:

```
{
    "StreamDescription": {
        "StreamStatus": "DELETING",
        "StreamName": "Foo",
        "StreamARN": "arn:aws:kinesis:us-west-2:account-id:stream/Foo",
        "Shards": []
    }
}
```

After the stream is fully deleted, describe-stream will result in a "not found" error:

```
A client error (ResourceNotFoundException) occurred when calling the DescribeStream operation:
Stream Foo under account 112233445566 not found.
```

Learning Amazon Kinesis Data Streams Development

These modules are designed to teach you what you need to know to become proficient in Kinesis Data Streams development. If you are unsure which streaming service is right for you, see the comparison information at What is Streaming Data?. Before you begin, be sure you are familiar with the concepts discussed in Amazon Kinesis Data Streams Key Concepts and Tutorial: Visualizing Web Traffic Using Amazon Kinesis Data Streams, particularly streams, shards, producers, and consumers. It is also helpful to have completed Tutorial: Visualizing Web Traffic Using Amazon Kinesis Data Streams and Tutorial: Getting Started With Amazon Kinesis Data Streams Using AWS CLI.

Topics

- Part One: Streams, Producers, and Consumers

Part One: Streams, Producers, and Consumers

This is Part One of a multi-part series to learn how to develop for Amazon Kinesis Data Streams in Java. If you are unsure which streaming service is right for you, see the comparison information at What is Streaming Data?.

The scenario for this module is to ingest stock trades into a stream and write a simple application that performs calculations on the stream. In Part One, you learn how to send a stream of records to Kinesis Data Streams and implement an application that consumes and processes the records in near real time. In subsequent parts of this series, the scenario is extended to include more intermediate and advanced design and programming considerations for the stock trade analysis model that apply to most Kinesis Data Streams business applications.

Important
After you create a stream, your account incurs nominal charges for Kinesis Data Streams usage because Kinesis Data Streams is not eligible for the AWS Free Tier. After the consumer application starts, it also incurs nominal charges for DynamoDB usage. DynamoDB is used by the consumer application to track processing state. When you are finished with this application, delete your AWS resources to stop incurring charges. For more information, see Step 7: Finishing Up.

The code does not access actual stock market data, but instead simulates the stream of stock trades. It does so by using a random stock trade generator that has a starting point of real market data for the top 25 stocks by market capitalization as of February 2015. If you have access to a real time stream of stock trades, you might be interested in deriving useful, timely statistics from that stream. For example, you might want to perform a sliding window analysis where you determine the most popular stock purchased in the last 5 minutes. Or you might want a notification whenever there is a sell order that is too large (that is, it has too many shares). The code shown in this series can be extended to provide such functionality.

You can work through the steps in this module on your desktop or laptop and run both the producer and consumer code on the same machine or any platform that supports the defined requirements, such as Amazon EC2.

The examples shown use the US West (Oregon) Region, but they work on any of the Regions that support Kinesis Data Streams.

Topics

- Prerequisites
- Step 1: Create a Stream
- Step 2: Create IAM Policy and User
- Step 3: Download and Build Implementation Code
- Step 4: Implement the Producer
- Step 5: Implement the Consumer
- Step 6: (Optional) Extending the Consumer
- Step 7: Finishing Up

Prerequisites

Amazon Web Services Account

Before you begin, be sure you are familiar with the concepts discussed in Amazon Kinesis Data Streams Key Concepts and Tutorial: Visualizing Web Traffic Using Amazon Kinesis Data Streams, particularly streams, shards, producers, and consumers. It is also helpful to have completed Tutorial: Visualizing Web Traffic Using Amazon Kinesis Data Streams and Tutorial: Getting Started With Amazon Kinesis Data Streams Using AWS CLI.

You need an AWS account and a web browser to access the AWS Management Console.

For console access, use your IAM user name and password to sign in to the AWS Management Console using the IAM sign-in page. IAM lets you securely control access to AWS services and resources in your AWS account. For more information about creating access keys, see How Do I Get Security Credentials? in the *AWS General Reference.*

For more information about IAM and security key setup instructions, see Create an IAM User.

System Software Requirements

The system used to run the application must have Java 7 or higher installed. To download and install the latest JDK, go to Oracle's Java SE installation site.

If you have a Java IDE, such as Eclipse, you can open the source code, edit, build, and run it.

You need the latest AWS SDK for Java version. If you are using Eclipse as your IDE, you can install the AWS Toolkit for Eclipse instead.

The consumer app requires the Kinesis Client Library (KCL) version 1.2.1 or higher, which you can obtain from GitHub at Kinesis Client Library (Java).

Step 1: Create a Stream

In this step, you create the stream you'll be using in subsequent steps.

To create a stream

1. Open the Kinesis console at https://console.aws.amazon.com/kinesis.

2. Choose **Go to the Streams console**.

3. In the navigation bar, expand the Region selector and choose a Region.

4. Choose **Create Kinesis stream**.

5. Type a name for your stream (for example, **StockTradeStream**).

6. Type **1** for the number of shards, but leave **Estimate the number of shards you'll need** collapsed.

7. Choose **Create Kinesis stream**.

On the **Kinesis streams** list page, the status of your stream is `CREATING` while the stream is being created. When the stream is ready to use, the status changes to `ACTIVE`. Choose the name of your stream. In the page that appears, the **Details** tab displays a summary of your stream configuration. The **Monitoring** section displays monitoring information for the stream.

Additional Information About Shards

When you begin to use Kinesis Data Streams outside of this learning module, you may need to plan the stream creation process more carefully. You should plan for expected maximum demand when you provision shards. Using this scenario as an example, U.S. stock market trading traffic peaks during the day (Eastern time) and demand estimates should be sampled from that time of day. You then have a choice to provision for the maximum expected demand, or scale your stream up and down in response to demand fluctuations.

A *shard* is a unit of throughput capacity. On the **Create Kinesis stream** page, expand **Estimate the number of shards you'll need**. Type the average record size, the maximum records written per second, and the number of consuming applications, using the following guidelines:

Average record size
An estimate of the calculated average size of your records. If you don't know this value, use the estimated maximum record size for this value.

Max records written
Take into account the number of entities providing data and the approximate number of records per second produced by each. For example, if you are getting stock trade data from 20 trading servers and each generates 250 trades per second, the total number of trades (records) per second is 5000/second.

Number of consuming applications
The number of applications that independently read from the stream to process the stream in a different way and produce different output. Each application can have multiple instances running on different machines (i.e., run in a cluster) so that it can keep up with a high volume stream.

If the estimated shards shown exceeds your current shard limit, you may need to submit a request to increase that limit before you can create a stream with that number of shards. To request an increase to your shard limit, use the Kinesis Data Streams Limits form. For more information about streams and shards, see Kinesis Data Streams and Managing Kinesis Data Streams Using Java.

Step 2: Create IAM Policy and User

Security best practices for AWS dictate the use of fine-grained permissions to control access to different resources. AWS Identity and Access Management allows you to manage users and user permissions in AWS. An IAM policy explicitly lists actions which are allowed and the resources on which the actions are applicable.

The following are the minimum permissions generally required for a Kinesis Data Streams producer and consumer.

Producer

Actions	Resource	Purpose
DescribeStream	Kinesis data stream	Before attempting to write records, the producer should check if the stream exists and is active.
PutRecord, PutRecords	Kinesis data stream	Write records to Kinesis Data Streams.

Consumer

Actions	Resource	Purpose
DescribeStream	Kinesis data stream	Before attempting to read records, the consumer checks if the stream exists and is active, and if the shards are contained in the stream.
GetRecords, GetShardIterator	Kinesis data stream	Read records from a Kinesis Data Streams shard.
CreateTable, DescribeTable, GetItem, PutItem, Scan, UpdateItem	Amazon DynamoDB table	If the consumer is developed using the Kinesis Client Library (KCL), it needs permissions to a DynamoDB table to track the processing state of the application. The first consumer started creates the table.
DeleteItem	Amazon DynamoDB table	For when the consumer performs split/merge operations on Kinesis Data Streams shards.
PutMetricData	Amazon CloudWatch log	The KCL also uploads metrics to CloudWatch, which are useful for monitoring the application.

For this application, you create a single IAM policy that grants all of the above permissions. In practice, you might want to consider creating two policies, one for producers and one for consumers. The policies you set up here are re-usable in subsequent learning modules in this series.

To create an IAM policy

1. Locate the Amazon Resource Name (ARN) for the new stream. You can find this ARN listed as **Stream ARN** at the top of the **Details** tab. The ARN format is as follows:

```
1  arn:aws:kinesis:region:account:stream/name
```

region
The Region code; for example, `us-west-2`. For more information, see Region and Availability Zone Concepts.
account
The AWS account ID, as shown in Account Settings.
name
The name of the stream from Step 1: Create a Stream, which is `StockTradeStream`.

1. Determine the ARN for the DynamoDB table to be used by the consumer (and created by the first consumer instance). It must be in the following format:

```
1  arn:aws:dynamodb:region:account:table/name
```

   The Region and account are from the same place as the previous step, but this time *name* is the name of the table created and used by the consumer application. The KCL used by the consumer uses the application name as the table name. Use `StockTradesProcessor`, which is the application name used later.

2. In the IAM console, in **Policies** (https://console.aws.amazon.com/iam/home#policies), choose **Create policy**. If this is the first time that you have worked with IAM policies, choose **Get Started**, **Create Policy**.

3. Choose **Select** next to **Policy Generator**.

4. Choose **Amazon Kinesis** as the AWS service.

5. Select `DescribeStream`, `GetShardIterator`, `GetRecords`, `PutRecord`, and `PutRecords` as the allowed actions.

6. Type the ARN that you created in Step 1.

7. Use **Add Statement** for each of the following:
   [See the AWS documentation website for more details]

   The asterisk (∗) that is used when specifying an ARN is not required. In this case, it's because there is no specific resource in CloudWatch on which the `PutMetricData` action is invoked.

8. Choose **Next Step**.

9. Change **Policy Name** to `StockTradeStreamPolicy`, review the code, and choose **Create Policy**.

The resulting policy document should look something like the following:

```
1  {
2    "Version": "2012-10-17",
3    "Statement": [
4      {
5        "Sid": "Stmt123",
6        "Effect": "Allow",
7        "Action": [
8          "kinesis:DescribeStream",
9          "kinesis:PutRecord",
10         "kinesis:PutRecords",
11         "kinesis:GetShardIterator",
12         "kinesis:GetRecords"
13       ],
14       "Resource": [
15         "arn:aws:kinesis:us-west-2:123:stream/StockTradeStream"
16       ]
17     },
```

```
18    {
19      "Sid": "Stmt456",
20      "Effect": "Allow",
21      "Action": [
22        "dynamodb:*"
23      ],
24      "Resource": [
25        "arn:aws:dynamodb:us-west-2:123:table/StockTradesProcessor"
26      ]
27    },
28    {
29      "Sid": "Stmt789",
30      "Effect": "Allow",
31      "Action": [
32        "cloudwatch:PutMetricData"
33      ],
34      "Resource": [
35        "*"
36      ]
37    }
38  ]
39 }
```

To create an IAM user

1. Open the IAM console at https://console.aws.amazon.com/iam/.

2. On the **Users** page, choose **Add user**.

3. For **User name**, type StockTradeStreamUser.

4. For **Access type**, choose **Programmatic access**, and then choose **Next: Permissions**.

5. Choose **Attach existing policies directly**.

6. Search by name for the policy that you created. Select the box to the left of the policy name, and then choose **Next: Review**.

7. Review the details and summary, and then choose **Create user**.

8. Copy the **Access key ID**, and save it privately. Under **Secret access key**, choose **Show**, and save that key privately also.

9. Paste the access and secret keys to a local file in a safe place that only you can access. For this application, create a file named ~/.aws/credentials (with strict permissions). The file should be in the following format:

```
1 [default]
2 aws_access_key_id=access key
3 aws_secret_access_key=secret access key
```

To attach an IAM policy to a user

1. In the IAM console, open Policies and choose **Policy Actions**.

2. Choose StockTradeStreamPolicy and **Attach**.

3. Choose StockTradeStreamUser and **Attach Policy**.

Step 3: Download and Build Implementation Code

Skeleton code has been provided for you, containing a stub implementation for both the stock trade stream ingestion (*producer*) as well as the processing of the data (*consumer*). The following procedure shows how to complete the implementations.

To download and build the implementation code

1. Download the source code on to your computer.

2. Create a project in your favorite IDE with the source code, adhering to the provided folder structure.

3. Add the following libraries to the project:
   - Amazon Kinesis Client Library (KCL)
   - AWS SDK
   - Apache HttpCore
   - Apache HttpClient
   - Apache Commons Lang
   - Apache Commons Logging
   - Guava (Google Core Libraries For Java)
   - Jackson Annotations
   - Jackson Core
   - Jackson Databind
   - Jackson Dataformat: CBOR
   - Joda Time

4. Depending on your IDE, the project might be built automatically. If not, build the project using the appropriate steps for your IDE.

If you complete these steps successfully, you are now ready to move to the next section. If your build generates errors at any stage, you need to investigate and fix them before proceeding.

Step 4: Implement the Producer

This application uses the real-world scenario of stock market trade monitoring. The following principles briefly explain how this scenario maps to the producer and supporting code structure.

Refer to the source code and review the following information.

StockTrade class

An individual stock trade is represented by an instance of the `StockTrade` class, which contains attributes such as the ticker symbol, price, number of shares, the type of the trade (buy or sell), and an ID uniquely identifying the trade. This class is implemented for you.

Stream record

A stream is a sequence of records. A record is a serialization of a `StockTrade` instance in JSON format. For example:

```
1  {
2    "tickerSymbol": "AMZN",
3    "tradeType": "BUY",
4    "price": 395.87,
5    "quantity": 16,
6    "id": 3567129045
7  }
```

StockTradeGenerator class

`StockTradeGenerator` has a method called `getRandomTrade()` that returns a new randomly generated stock trade every time it is invoked. This class is implemented for you.

StockTradesWriter class

The `main` method of the producer, `StockTradesWriter` continuously retrieves a random trade and then sends it to Kinesis Data Streams by performing the following tasks:

1. Reads the stream name and Region name as input.

2. Creates an `AmazonKinesisClientBuilder`.

3. Uses the client builder to set the Region, credentials, and client configuration.

4. Builds an `AmazonKinesis` client using the client builder.

5. Checks that the stream exists and is active (if not, it exits with an error).

6. In a continuous loop, calls the `StockTradeGenerator.getRandomTrade()` method and then the `sendStockTrade` method to send the trade to the stream every 100 milliseconds. The `sendStockTrade` method of the `StockTradesWriter` class has the following code:

```
1  private static void sendStockTrade(StockTrade trade, AmazonKinesis kinesisClient, String
       streamName) {
2      byte[] bytes = trade.toJsonAsBytes();
3      // The bytes could be null if there is an issue with the JSON serialization by the Jackson
           JSON library.
4      if (bytes == null) {
5          LOG.warn("Could not get JSON bytes for stock trade");
6          return;
7      }
8
9      LOG.info("Putting trade: " + trade.toString());
10     PutRecordRequest putRecord = new PutRecordRequest();
11     putRecord.setStreamName(streamName);
```

```
12    // We use the ticker symbol as the partition key, explained in the Supplemental Information
          section below.
13    putRecord.setPartitionKey(trade.getTickerSymbol());
14    putRecord.setData(ByteBuffer.wrap(bytes));
15
16    try {
17        kinesisClient.putRecord(putRecord);
18    } catch (AmazonClientException ex) {
19        LOG.warn("Error sending record to Amazon Kinesis.", ex);
20    }
21 }
```

Refer to the following code breakdown:

- The PutRecord API expects a byte array, and you need to convert trade to JSON format. This single line of code performs that operation:

```
1 byte[] bytes = trade.toJsonAsBytes();
```

- Before you can send the trade, you create a new PutRecordRequest instance (called putRecord in this case):

```
1 PutRecordRequest putRecord = new PutRecordRequest();
```

  Each PutRecord call requires the stream name, partition key, and data blob. The following code populates these fields in the putRecord object using its setXxxx() methods:

```
1 putRecord.setStreamName(streamName);
2 putRecord.setPartitionKey(trade.getTickerSymbol());
3 putRecord.setData(ByteBuffer.wrap(bytes));
```

  The example uses a stock ticket as a partition key, which maps the record to a specific shard. In practice, you should have hundreds or thousands of partition keys per shard such that records are evenly dispersed across your stream. For more information about how to add data to a stream, see Adding Data to a Stream.

  Now putRecord is ready to send to the client (the put operation):

```
1 kinesisClient.putRecord(putRecord);
```

- Error checking and logging are always useful additions. This code logs error conditions:

```
1 if (bytes == null) {
2    LOG.warn("Could not get JSON bytes for stock trade");
3    return;
4 }
```

  Add the try/catch block around the put operation:

```
1 try {
2        kinesisClient.putRecord(putRecord);
3 } catch (AmazonClientException ex) {
4        LOG.warn("Error sending record to Amazon Kinesis.", ex);
5 }
```

  This is because a Kinesis Data Streams put operation can fail because of a network error, or due to the stream reaching its throughput limits and getting throttled. We recommend carefully considering your retry policy for put operations to avoid data loss, such using as a simple retry.

- Status logging is helpful but optional:

47

```
1 LOG.info("Putting trade: " + trade.toString());
```

The producer shown here uses the Kinesis Data Streams API single record functionality, `PutRecord`. In practice, if an individual producer is generating a lot of records, it is often more efficient to use the multiple records functionality of `PutRecords` and send batches of records at a time. For more information, see Adding Data to a Stream.

To run the producer

1. Verify that the access key and secret key pair retrieved earlier (when creating the IAM user) are saved in the file `~/.aws/credentials`.

2. Run the `StockTradeWriter` class with the following arguments:

```
1 StockTradeStream us-west-2
```

If you created your stream in a Region other than `us-west-2`, you have to specify that Region here instead.

You should see output similar to the following:

```
1 Feb 16, 2015 3:53:00 PM
2 com.amazonaws.services.kinesis.samples.stocktrades.writer.StockTradesWriter sendStockTrade
3 INFO: Putting trade: ID 8: SELL 996 shares of BUD for $124.18
4 Feb 16, 2015 3:53:00 PM
5 com.amazonaws.services.kinesis.samples.stocktrades.writer.StockTradesWriter sendStockTrade
6 INFO: Putting trade: ID 9: BUY 159 shares of GE for $20.85
7 Feb 16, 2015 3:53:01 PM
8 com.amazonaws.services.kinesis.samples.stocktrades.writer.StockTradesWriter sendStockTrade
9 INFO: Putting trade: ID 10: BUY 322 shares of WMT for $90.08
```

Your stock trade stream is now being ingested by Kinesis Data Streams.

Step 5: Implement the Consumer

The consumer application you are developing continuously processes the stock trades stream that you created in Step 4: Implement the Producer, and outputs the most popular stocks being bought and sold every minute. The application is built on top of the KCL, which does a lot of the heavy lifting common to consumer apps. For more information, see Developing Amazon Kinesis Data Streams Consumers Using the Kinesis Client Library.

Refer to the source code and review the following information.

StockTradesProcessor class

Main class of the consumer, provided for you, which performs the following tasks:

- Read the application, stream, and Region names, passed in as arguments.
- Read credentials from `~/.aws/credentials`.
- Create a `RecordProcessorFactory` instance that serves instances of `RecordProcessor`, implemented by a `StockTradeRecordProcessor` instance.
- Create a KCL worker with the `RecordProcessorFactory` instance and a standard configuration including the stream name, credentials, and application name.
- The worker creates a new thread for each shard (assigned to this consumer instance), which continuously loops to read records from Kinesis Data Streams and then invokes the `RecordProcessor` instance to process each batch of records received.

StockTradeRecordProcessor class

Implementation of the `RecordProcessor` instance, which in turn implements three required methods: `initialize`, `processRecords`, and `shutdown`.

As the names suggest, `initialize` and `shutdown` are used by KCL to let the record processor know when it should be ready to start receiving records and when it should expect to stop receiving records, respectively, so it can do any application-specific setup and termination tasks. The code for these is provided for you. The main processing happens in the `processRecords` method, which in turn uses `processRecord` for each record. This latter method is provided as mostly empty skeleton code for you to implement in the next step, where it is explained further.

Also of note is the implementation of support methods for `processRecord`: `reportStats`, and `resetStats`, which are empty in the original source code.

The `processsRecords` method is implemented for you, and performs the following steps:

- For each record passed in, call `processRecord` on it.
- If at least 1 minute has elapsed since the last report, call `reportStats()` which prints out the latest stats, and then `resetStats()` which clears the stats so that the next interval includes only new records.
- Set the next reporting time.
- If at least 1 minute has elapsed since the last checkpoint, call `checkpoint()`.
- Set the next checkpointing time. This method uses 60-second intervals for the reporting and checkpointing rate. For more information about checkpointing, see Additional Information About the Consumer.

StockStats class

This class provides data retention and statistics tracking for the most popular stocks over time. This code is provided for you and contains the following methods:

- `addStockTrade(StockTrade)`: Injects the given `StockTrade` into the running statistics.
- `toString()`: Returns the statistics in a formatted string. The way this class keeps track of the most popular stock is that it keeps a running count of the total number of trades for each stock and the maximum count. It keeps these counts updated whenever a stock trade arrives.

Add code to the methods of the `StockTradeRecordProcessor` class, as shown in the following steps.

To implement the consumer

1. Implement the `processRecord` method by instantiating a correctly sized `StockTrade` object and adding the record data to it, logging a warning if there's a problem.

```
1 StockTrade trade = StockTrade.fromJsonAsBytes(record.getData().array());
2 if (trade == null) {
3    LOG.warn("Skipping record. Unable to parse record into StockTrade. Partition Key: " +
         record.getPartitionKey());
4    return;
5 }
6 stockStats.addStockTrade(trade);
```

2. Implement a simple `reportStats` method. Feel free to modify the output format to your preferences.

```
1 System.out.println("****** Shard " + kinesisShardId + " stats for last 1 minute ******\n" +
2                    stockStats + "\n" +
3                    "***********************************************************\n");
```

3. Finally, implement the `resetStats` method, which creates a new `stockStats` instance.

```
1 stockStats = new StockStats();
```

To run the consumer

1. Run the producer you wrote in the previous module to inject simulated stock trade records into your stream.

2. Verify that the access key and secret key pair retrieved earlier (when creating the IAM user) are saved in the file `~/.aws/credentials` .

3. Run the `StockTradesProcessor` class with the following arguments:

```
1 StockTradesProcessor StockTradeStream us-west-2
```

Note that if you created your stream in a Region other than `us-west-2`, you have to specify that Region here instead.

After a minute, you should see output like the following, refreshed every minute thereafter:

```
1  ****** Shard shardId-000000000001 stats for last 1 minute ******
2  Most popular stock being bought: WMT, 27 buys.
3  Most popular stock being sold: PTR, 14 sells.
4  ***********************************************************
```

Additional Information About the Consumer

If you are familiar with the advantages of the KCL, discussed in Developing Amazon Kinesis Data Streams Consumers Using the Kinesis Client Library and elsewhere, you may be wondering why you should use it here. Although you use only a single shard stream and a single consumer instance to process it, it is still easier to implement the consumer with the KCL. Compare the code implementation steps in the producer section to the consumer, and you can see the comparative ease of implementing a consumer. This is largely due to the services that the KCL provides.

In this application, you focus on implementing a record processor class that can process individual records. You don't have to worry about how the records are fetched from Kinesis Data Streams; The KCL fetches the records and invoke the record processor whenever there are new records available. Also, you don't have to worry about how many shards and consumer instances there are; if the stream is scaled up, you don't have to rewrite your application to handle more than one shard or one consumer instance.

The term *checkpointing* means recording the point in the stream up to the data records that have been consumed and processed thus far, so that if the application crashes, the stream is read from that point and not from the beginning of the stream. The subject of checkpointing and the various design patterns and best practices for it are outside the scope of this chapter, but is something you may be confronted with in production environments.

As you learned in Step 4: Implement the Producer, the `put` operations in the Kinesis Data Streams API take a *partition key* as input. A partition key is used by Kinesis Data Streams as a mechanism to split records across multiple shards (when there is more than one shard in the stream). The same partition key always routes to the same shard. This allows the consumer that processes a particular shard to be designed with the assumption that records with the same partition key would only be sent to that consumer, and no records with the same partition key would end up at any other consumer. Therefore, a consumer's worker can aggregate all records with the same partition key without worrying that it might be missing needed data.

In this application, the consumer's processing of records is not intensive, so you can use one shard and do the processing in the same thread as the KCL thread. In practice, however, consider first scaling up the number of shards, as the next module in this learning series demonstrates. In some cases you may want to switch processing to a different thread, or use a thread pool if your record processing is expected to be intensive. In this way, the KCL can fetch new records more quickly while the other threads can process the records in parallel. Note that multithreaded design is not trivial and should be approached with advanced techniques, so increasing your shard count is usually the most effective and easiest way to scale up.

Step 6: (Optional) Extending the Consumer

The application shown here may already be sufficient for your purposes. This optional section shows how you might want to extend the consumer code for a slightly more elaborate scenario.

If you want to know about the biggest sell orders each minute, this is a matter of modifying the `StockStats` class in three places to accommodate this new priority.

To extend the consumer

1. Add new instance variables:

```
// Ticker symbol of the stock that had the largest quantity of shares sold
private String largestSellOrderStock;
// Quantity of shares for the largest sell order trade
private long largestSellOrderQuantity;
```

2. Add the following code to `addStockTrade`:

```
if (type == TradeType.SELL) {
    if (largestSellOrderStock == null || trade.getQuantity() > largestSellOrderQuantity) {
        largestSellOrderStock = trade.getTickerSymbol();
        largestSellOrderQuantity = trade.getQuantity();
    }
}
```

3. Modify the `toString` method to print the additional information:

```
public String toString() {
    return String.format(
            "Most popular stock being bought: %s, %d buys.%n" +
            "Most popular stock being sold: %s, %d sells.%n" +
            "Largest sell order: %d shares of %s.",
            getMostPopularStock(TradeType.BUY), getMostPopularStockCount(TradeType.BUY),
            getMostPopularStock(TradeType.SELL), getMostPopularStockCount(TradeType.SELL),
            largestSellOrderQuantity, largestSellOrderStock);
}
```

If you run the consumer now (remember to run the producer also), you should see output similar to this:

```
****** Shard shardId-000000000001 stats for last 1 minute ******
Most popular stock being bought: WMT, 27 buys.
Most popular stock being sold: PTR, 14 sells.
Largest sell order: 996 shares of BUD.
****************************************************************
```

Step 7: Finishing Up

Because you are paying to use the Kinesis data stream, make sure you delete it and the corresponding DynamoDB table once you are done with it. Nominal charges occur on an active stream even when you aren't sending and getting records. This is because an active stream is using resources by continuously "listening" for incoming records and requests to get records.

To delete the stream and table

1. Shut down any producers and consumers that you may still have running.

2. Open the Kinesis console at https://console.aws.amazon.com/kinesis.

3. Choose the stream that you created for this application (`StockTradeStream`).

4. Choose **Delete Stream**.

5. Open the DynamoDB console at https://console.aws.amazon.com/dynamodb/.

6. Delete the `StockTradesProcessor` table.

Summary

Processing a large amount of data in near real time doesn't require writing any magical code or developing a huge infrastructure. It is as simple as writing logic to process a small amount of data (like writing `processRecord(Record)`) but using Kinesis Data Streams to scale so that it works for a large amount of streaming data. You don't have to worry about how your processing would scale because Kinesis Data Streams handles it for you. All you have to do is send your streaming records to Kinesis Data Streams and write the logic to process each new record received.

Here are some potential enhancements for this application.

Aggregate across all shards
Currently, you get stats resulting from aggregation of the data records received by a single worker from a single shard (a shard cannot be processed by more than one worker in a single application at the same time). Of course, when you scale and have more than one shard, you may want to aggregate across all shards. This can be done by having a pipeline architecture where the output of each worker is fed into another stream with a single shard, which is processed by a worker that aggregates the outputs of the first stage. Because the data from the first stage is limited (one sample per minute per shard), it would easily be handled by one shard.

Scale processing
When the stream scales up to have many shards (because many producers are sending data), the way to scale the processing is to add more workers. You can run the workers in EC2 instances and leverage Auto Scaling groups.

Leverage connectors to S3/DynamoDB/Redshift/Storm
As a stream is continuously processed, its output can be sent to other destinations. AWS provides connectors to integrate Kinesis Data Streams with other AWS services and third-party tools.

Next Steps

- For more information about using Kinesis Data Streams API operations, see Developing Amazon Kinesis Data Streams Producers Using the Amazon Kinesis Data Streams API with the AWS SDK for Java, Developing Amazon Kinesis Data Streams Consumers Using the Amazon Kinesis Data Streams API with the AWS SDK for Java, and Managing Kinesis Data Streams Using Java.
- For more information about Kinesis Client Library, see Developing Amazon Kinesis Data Streams Consumers Using the Kinesis Client Library.
- For more information about how to optimize your application, see Advanced Topics.

Working With Amazon Kinesis Data Streams

This documentation provides information about working with Amazon Kinesis Data Streams. If you are new to Kinesis Data Streams, start by becoming familiar with the concepts and terminology presented in What Is Amazon Kinesis Data Streams? and Getting Started Using Amazon Kinesis Data Streams.

Topics

- Writing Data To Amazon Kinesis Data Streams
- Reading Data From Amazon Kinesis Data Streams
- Managing Kinesis Data Streams Using Java
- Managing Kinesis Streams Using the Console
- Monitoring Amazon Kinesis Data Streams
- Tagging Your Streams in Amazon Kinesis Data Streams
- Controlling Access to Amazon Kinesis Data Streams Resources Using IAM
- Using Amazon Kinesis Data Streams with Interface VPC Endpoints
- Using Server-Side Encryption

Writing Data To Amazon Kinesis Data Streams

A *producer* is an application that writes data to Amazon Kinesis Data Streams. You can build producers for Kinesis Data Streams. If you are new to Kinesis Data Streams, start by becoming familiar with the concepts and terminology presented in What Is Amazon Kinesis Data Streams? and Getting Started Using Amazon Kinesis Data Streams.

Topics

- Developing Amazon Kinesis Data Streams Producers Using the Kinesis Producer Library
- Developing Amazon Kinesis Data Streams Producers Using the Amazon Kinesis Data Streams API with the AWS SDK for Java
- Writing to Amazon Kinesis Data Streams Using Kinesis Agent
- Troubleshooting Amazon Kinesis Data Streams Producers
- Advanced Topics for Amazon Kinesis Data Streams Producers

Developing Amazon Kinesis Data Streams Producers Using the Kinesis Producer Library

An Amazon Kinesis Data Streams producer is any application that puts user data records into a Kinesis data stream (also called *data ingestion*). The Kinesis Producer Library (KPL) simplifies producer application development, allowing developers to achieve high write throughput to a Kinesis data stream.

You can monitor the KPL with Amazon CloudWatch. For more information, see Monitoring the Kinesis Producer Library with Amazon CloudWatch.

Topics

- Role of the KPL
- Advantages of Using the KPL
- When Not to Use the KPL
- Installing the KPL
- Transitioning to Amazon Trust Services (ATS) Certificates for the Kinesis Producer Library
- KPL Supported Platforms
- KPL Key Concepts
- Integrating the KPL with Producer Code
- Writing to your Kinesis Data Stream Using the KPL
- Configuring the Kinesis Producer Library
- Consumer De-aggregation

Role of the KPL

The KPL is an easy-to-use, highly configurable library that helps you write to a Kinesis data stream. It acts as an intermediary between your producer application code and the Kinesis Data Streams API actions. The KPL performs the following primary tasks:

- Writes to one or more Kinesis data streams with an automatic and configurable retry mechanism
- Collects records and uses `PutRecords` to write multiple records to multiple shards per request
- Aggregates user records to increase payload size and improve throughput
- Integrates seamlessly with the Kinesis Client Library (KCL) to de-aggregate batched records on the consumer
- Submits Amazon CloudWatch metrics on your behalf to provide visibility into producer performance

Note that the KPL is different from the Kinesis Data Streams API that is available in the AWS SDKs. The Kinesis Data Streams API helps you manage many aspects of Kinesis Data Streams (including creating streams, resharding, and putting and getting records), while the KPL provides a layer of abstraction specifically for ingesting data. For information about the Kinesis Data Streams API, see the Amazon Kinesis API Reference.

Advantages of Using the KPL

The following list represents some of the major advantages to using the KPL for developing Kinesis Data Streams producers.

The KPL can be used in either synchronous or asynchronous use cases. We suggest using the higher performance of the asynchronous interface unless there is a specific reason to use synchronous behavior. For more information about these two use cases and example code, see Writing to your Kinesis Data Stream Using the KPL.

Performance Benefits
The KPL can help build high-performance producers. Consider a situation where your Amazon EC2 instances serve as a proxy for collecting 100-byte events from hundreds or thousands of low power devices and writing records into a Kinesis data stream. These EC2 instances must each write thousands of events per second to your

data stream. To achieve the throughput needed, producers must implement complicated logic, such as batching or multithreading, in addition to retry logic and record de-aggregation at the consumer side. The KPL performs all of these tasks for you.

Consumer-Side Ease of Use

For consumer-side developers using the KCL in Java, the KPL integrates without additional effort. When the KCL retrieves an aggregated Kinesis Data Streams record consisting of multiple KPL user records, it automatically invokes the KPL to extract the individual user records before returning them to the user.

For consumer-side developers who do not use the KCL but instead use the API operation `GetRecords` directly, a KPL Java library is available to extract the individual user records before returning them to the user.

Producer Monitoring

You can collect, monitor, and analyze your Kinesis Data Streams producers using Amazon CloudWatch and the KPL. The KPL emits throughput, error, and other metrics to CloudWatch on your behalf, and is configurable to monitor at the stream, shard, or producer level.

Asynchronous Architecture

Because the KPL may buffer records before sending them to Kinesis Data Streams, it does not force the caller application to block and wait for a confirmation that the record has arrived at the server before continuing execution. A call to put a record into the KPL always returns immediately and does not wait for the record to be sent or a response to be received from the server. Instead, a `Future` object is created that receives the result of sending the record to Kinesis Data Streams at a later time. This is the same behavior as asynchronous clients in the AWS SDK.

When Not to Use the KPL

The KPL can incur an additional processing delay of up to `RecordMaxBufferedTime` within the library (user-configurable). Larger values of `RecordMaxBufferedTime` results in higher packing efficiencies and better performance. Applications that cannot tolerate this additional delay may need to use the AWS SDK directly. For more information about using the AWS SDK with Kinesis Data Streams, see Developing Amazon Kinesis Data Streams Producers Using the Amazon Kinesis Data Streams API with the AWS SDK for Java. For more information about `RecordMaxBufferedTime` and other user-configurable properties of the KPL, see Configuring the Kinesis Producer Library.

Installing the KPL

Amazon provides pre-built binaries of the C++ Kinesis Producer Library (KPL) for macOS, Windows, and recent Linux distributions (for supported platform details, see the next section). These binaries are packaged as part of Java .jar files and are automatically invoked and used if you are using Maven to install the package. To locate the latest versions of the KPL and KCL, use the following Maven search links:

- KPL
- KCL

The Linux binaries have been compiled with the GNU Compiler Collection (GCC) and statically linked against libstdc++ on Linux. They are expected to work on any 64-bit Linux distribution that includes a glibc version 2.5 or higher.

Users of older Linux distributions can build the KPL using the build instructions provided along with the source on GitHub. To download the KPL from GitHub, see Kinesis Producer Library.

Transitioning to Amazon Trust Services (ATS) Certificates for the Kinesis Producer Library

On February 9, 2018, at 9:00 AM PST, Amazon Kinesis Data Streams installed ATS certificates. To continue to be able to write records to Kinesis Data Streams using the Kinesis Producer Library (KPL), you must upgrade your installation of the KPL to version 0.12.6 or later. This change affects all AWS Regions.

For information about the move to ATS, please see How to Prepare for AWS's Move to Its Own Certificate Authority.

If you encounter problems and need technical support, create a case with the AWS Support Center.

KPL Supported Platforms

The Kinesis Producer Library (KPL) is written in C++ and runs as a child process to the main user process. Precompiled 64-bit native binaries are bundled with the Java release and are managed by the Java wrapper.

The Java package runs without the need to install any additional libraries on the following operating systems:

- Linux distributions with kernel 2.6.18 (September 2006) and later
- Apple OS X 10.9 and later
- Windows Server 2008 and later

Note that the KPL is 64-bit only.

Source Code

If the binaries provided in the KPL installation are not sufficient for your environment, the core of the KPL is written as a C++ module. The source code for the C++ module and the Java interface are released under the Amazon Public License and are available on GitHub at Kinesis Producer Library. Although the KPL can be used on any platform for which a recent standards-compliant C++ compiler and JRE are available, Amazon doesn't officially support any platform that is not on the supported platforms list.

KPL Key Concepts

The following sections contain concepts and terminology necessary to understand and benefit from the Kinesis Producer Library (KPL).

Topics

- Records
- Batching
- Aggregation
- Collection

Records

In this guide, we distinguish between *KPL user records* and *Kinesis Data Streams records*. When we use the term *record* without a qualifier, we refer to a *KPL user record*. When we refer to a Kinesis Data Streams record, we explicitly say *Kinesis Data Streams record*.

A KPL user record is a blob of data that has particular meaning to the user. Examples include a JSON blob representing a UI event on a website, or a log entry from a web server.

A Kinesis Data Streams record is an instance of the `Record` data structure defined by the Kinesis Data Streams service API. It contains a partition key, sequence number, and a blob of data.

Batching

Batching refers to performing a single action on multiple items instead of repeatedly performing the action on each individual item.

In this context, the "item" is a record, and the action is sending it to Kinesis Data Streams. In a non-batching situation, you would place each record in a separate Kinesis Data Streams record and make one HTTP request to send it to Kinesis Data Streams. With batching, each HTTP request can carry multiple records instead of just one.

The KPL supports two types of batching:

- *Aggregation* – Storing multiple records within a single Kinesis Data Streams record.
- *Collection* – Using the API operation `PutRecords` to send multiple Kinesis Data Streams records to one or more shards in your Kinesis data stream.

The two types of KPL batching are designed to coexist and can be turned on or off independently of one another. By default, both are turned on.

Aggregation

Aggregation refers to the storage of multiple records in a Kinesis Data Streams record. Aggregation allows customers to increase the number of records sent per API call, which effectively increases producer throughput.

Kinesis Data Streams shards support up to 1,000 Kinesis Data Streams records per second, or 1 MB throughput. The Kinesis Data Streams records per second limit binds customers with records smaller than 1 KB. Record aggregation allows customers to combine multiple records into a single Kinesis Data Streams record. This allows customers to improve their per shard throughput.

Consider the case of one shard in region us-east-1 that is currently running at a constant rate of 1,000 records per second, with records that are 512 bytes each. With KPL aggregation, you can pack 1,000 records into only 10 Kinesis Data Streams records, reducing the RPS to 10 (at 50 KB each).

Collection

Collection refers to batching multiple Kinesis Data Streams records and sending them in a single HTTP request with a call to the API operation `PutRecords`, instead of sending each Kinesis Data Streams record in its own HTTP request.

This increases throughput compared to using no collection because it reduces the overhead of making many separate HTTP requests. In fact, `PutRecords` itself was specifically designed for this purpose.

Collection differs from aggregation in that it is working with groups of Kinesis Data Streams records. The Kinesis Data Streams records being collected can still contain multiple records from the user. The relationship can be visualized as such:

```
1  record 0 --|
2  record 1   |            [ Aggregation ]
3     ...      |--> Amazon Kinesis record 0 --|
4     ...      |                              |
5  record A --|                               |
6                                             |
7     ...                    ...              |
8                                             |
9  record K --|                               |
10 record L   |                               |      [ Collection ]
11    ...      |--> Amazon Kinesis record C --|--> PutRecords Request
12    ...      |                              |
13 record S --|                               |
14                                            |
15    ...                    ...              |
16                                            |
17 record AA--|                               |
18 record BB  |                               |
19    ...      |--> Amazon Kinesis record M --|
20    ...      |
21 record ZZ--|
```

Integrating the KPL with Producer Code

The Kinesis Producer Library (KPL) runs in a separate process, and communicates with your parent user process using IPC. This architecture is sometimes called a microservice, and is chosen for two main reasons:

1) Your user process will not crash even if the KPL crashes
Your process could have tasks unrelated to Kinesis Data Streams, and may be able to continue operation even if the KPL crashes. It is also possible for your parent user process to restart the KPL and recover to a fully working state (this functionality is in the official wrappers).

An example is a web server that sends metrics to Kinesis Data Streams; the server can continue serving pages even if the Kinesis Data Streams part has stopped working. Crashing the whole server because of a bug in the KPL would therefore cause an unnecessary outage.

2) Arbitrary clients can be supported
There are always customers who use languages other than the ones officially supported. These customers should also be able to use the KPL easily.

Recommended Usage Matrix

The following usage matrix enumerates the recommended settings for different users and advises you about whether and how you should use the KPL. Keep in mind that if aggregation is enabled, de-aggregation must also be used to extract your records on the consumer side.

Producer side language	Consumer side language	KCL Version	Checkpoint logic	Can you use the KPL?	Caveats
Anything but Java	*	*	*	No	N/A
Java	Java	Uses Java SDK directly	N/A	Yes	If aggregation is used, you have to use the provided de-aggregation library after GetRecords calls.
Java	Anything but Java	Uses SDK directly	N/A	Yes	Must disable aggregation.
Java	Java	1.3.x	N/A	Yes	Must disable aggregation.
Java	Java	1.4.x	Calls checkpoint without any arguments	Yes	None
Java	Java	1.4.x	Calls checkpoint with an explicit sequence number	Yes	Either disable aggregation, or change the code to use extended sequence numbers for checkpointing.

Producer side language	Consumer side language	KCL Version	Checkpoint logic	Can you use the KPL?	Caveats
Java	Anything but Java	1.3.x + Multilanguage daemon + language-specific wrapper	N/A	Yes	Must disable aggregation.

Writing to your Kinesis Data Stream Using the KPL

The following sections show sample code in a progression from the simplest possible "bare-bones" producer on through to fully asynchronous code.

Barebones Producer Code

The following code is all that is needed to write a minimal working producer. The Kinesis Producer Library (KPL) user records are processed in the background.

```
1  // KinesisProducer gets credentials automatically like
2  // DefaultAWSCredentialsProviderChain.
3  // It also gets region automatically from the EC2 metadata service.
4  KinesisProducer kinesis = new KinesisProducer();
5  // Put some records
6  for (int i = 0; i < 100; ++i) {
7      ByteBuffer data = ByteBuffer.wrap("myData".getBytes("UTF-8"));
8      // doesn't block
9      kinesis.addUserRecord("myStream", "myPartitionKey", data);
10 }
11 // Do other stuff ...
```

Responding to Results Synchronously

In the previous example, the code didn't check whether the KPL user records succeeded. The KPL performs any retries needed to account for failures. But if you want to check on the results, you can examine them using the `Future` objects that are returned from **addUserRecord**, as in the following example (previous example shown for context):

```
1  KinesisProducer kinesis = new KinesisProducer();
2
3  // Put some records and save the Futures
4  List<Future<UserRecordResult>> putFutures = new LinkedList<Future<UserRecordResult>>();
5  for (int i = 0; i < 100; i++) {
6      ByteBuffer data = ByteBuffer.wrap("myData".getBytes("UTF-8"));
7      // doesn't block
8      putFutures.add(
9          kinesis.addUserRecord("myStream", "myPartitionKey", data));
10 }
11
12 // Wait for puts to finish and check the results
13 for (Future<UserRecordResult> f : putFutures) {
14     UserRecordResult result = f.get(); // this does block
15     if (result.isSuccess()) {
16         System.out.println("Put record into shard " +
17                              result.getShardId());
18     } else {
19         for (Attempt attempt : result.getAttempts()) {
20             // Analyze and respond to the failure
21         }
22     }
23 }
```

Responding to Results Asynchronously

The previous example is calling get() on a Future object, which blocks execution. If you don't want to block execution, you can use an asynchronous callback, as shown in the following example:

```
1  KinesisProducer kinesis = new KinesisProducer();
2
3  FutureCallback<UserRecordResult> myCallback = new FutureCallback<UserRecordResult>() {
4      @Override public void onFailure(Throwable t) {
5          /* Analyze and respond to the failure  */
6      };
7      @Override public void onSuccess(UserRecordResult result) {
8          /* Respond to the success */
9      };
10 };
11
12 for (int i = 0; i < 100; ++i) {
13     ByteBuffer data = ByteBuffer.wrap("myData".getBytes("UTF-8"));
14     ListenableFuture<UserRecordResult> f = kinesis.addUserRecord("myStream", "myPartitionKey",
           data);
15     // If the Future is complete by the time we call addCallback, the callback will be invoked
           immediately.
16     Futures.addCallback(f, myCallback);
17 }
```

Configuring the Kinesis Producer Library

Although the default settings should work well for most use cases, you may want to change some of the default settings to tailor the behavior of the KinesisProducer to your needs. An instance of the KinesisProducerConfiguration class can be passed to the KinesisProducer constructor to do so, for example:

```
1 KinesisProducerConfiguration config = new KinesisProducerConfiguration()
2          .setRecordMaxBufferedTime(3000)
3          .setMaxConnections(1)
4          .setRequestTimeout(60000)
5          .setRegion("us-west-1");
6
7 final KinesisProducer kinesisProducer = new KinesisProducer(config);
```

You can also load a configuration from a properties file:

```
1 KinesisProducerConfiguration config = KinesisProducerConfiguration.fromPropertiesFile("
      default_config.properties");
```

You can substitute any path and file name that the user process has access to. You can additionally call set methods on the KinesisProducerConfiguration instance created this way to customize the config.

The properties file should specify parameters using their names in PascalCase. The names match those used in the set methods in the KinesisProducerConfiguration class. For example:

```
1 RecordMaxBufferedTime = 100
2 MaxConnections = 4
3 RequestTimeout = 6000
4 Region = us-west-1
```

For more information about configuration parameter usage rules and value limits, see the sample configuration properties file on GitHub.

Note that after KinesisProducer is initialized, changing the KinesisProducerConfiguration instance that was used has no further effect. KinesisProducer does not currently support dynamic reconfiguration.

Consumer De-aggregation

Beginning with release 1.4.0, the KCL supports automatic de-aggregation of KPL user records. Consumer application code written with previous versions of the KCL will compile without any modification after you update the KCL. However, if KPL aggregation is being used on the producer side, there is a subtlety involving checkpointing: all subrecords within an aggregated record have the same sequence number, so additional data has to be stored with the checkpoint if you need to distinguish between subrecords. This additional data is referred to as the *subsequence number*.

Migrating from Previous Versions of the KCL

You are not required to change your existing calls to do checkpointing in conjunction with aggregation. It is still guaranteed that you can retrieve all records successfully stored in Kinesis Data Streams. The KCL now provides two new checkpoint operations to support particular use cases, described below.

In the event that your existing code was written for the KCL prior to KPL support, and your checkpoint operation is called without arguments, it is equivalent to checkpointing the sequence number of the last KPL user record in the batch. If your checkpoint operation is called with a sequence number string, it is equivalent to checkpointing the given sequence number of the batch along with the implicit subsequence number 0 (zero).

Calling the new KCL checkpoint operation `checkpoint()` without any arguments is semantically equivalent to checkpointing the sequence number of the last `Record` call in the batch, along with the implicit subsequence number 0 (zero).

Calling the new KCL checkpoint operation `checkpoint(Record record)` is semantically equivalent to checkpointing the given `Record`'s sequence number along with the implicit subsequence number 0 (zero). If the `Record` call is actually a `UserRecord`, the `UserRecord` sequence number and subsequence number are checkpointed.

Calling the new KCL checkpoint operation `checkpoint(String sequenceNumber, long subSequenceNumber)` explicitly checkpoints the given sequence number along with the given subsequence number.

In any of these cases, after the checkpoint is stored in the Amazon DynamoDB checkpoint table, the KCL can correctly resume retrieving records even when the application crashes and restarts. If more records are contained within the sequence, retrieval occurs starting with the next subsequence number record within the record with the most recently checkpointed sequence number. If the most recent checkpoint included the very last subsequence number of the previous sequence number record, retrieval occurs starting with the record with the next sequence number.

The next section discusses details of sequence and subsequence checkpointing for consumers that need to avoid skipping and duplication of records. If skipping (or duplication) of records when stopping and restarting your consumer's record processing is not important, you can run your existing code with no modification.

KCL Extensions for KPL De-aggregation

As previously discussed, KPL de-aggregation can involve subsequence checkpointing. To facilitate using subsequence checkpointing, a `UserRecord` class has been added to the KCL:

```
public class UserRecord extends Record {
    public long getSubSequenceNumber() {
    /* ... */
    }
    @Override
    public int hashCode() {
    /* contract-satisfying implementation */
    }
    @Override
```

```
10     public boolean equals(Object obj) {
11     /* contract-satisfying implementation */
12     }
13 }
```

This class is now used instead of `Record`. This does not break existing code because it is a subclass of `Record`. The `UserRecord` class represents both actual subrecords and standard, non-aggregated records. Non-aggregated records can be thought of as aggregated records with exactly one subrecord.

In addition, two new operations are added to`IRecordProcessorCheckpointer`:

```
1 public void checkpoint(Record record);
2 public void checkpoint(String sequenceNumber, long subSequenceNumber);
```

To begin using subsequence number checkpointing, you can perform the following conversion. Change the following form code:

```
1 checkpointer.checkpoint(record.getSequenceNumber());
```

New form code:

```
1 checkpointer.checkpoint(record);
```

We recommend that you use the `checkpoint(Record record)` form for subsequence checkpointing. However, if you are already storing `sequenceNumbers` in strings to use for checkpointing, you should now also store `subSequenceNumber`, as shown in the following example:

```
1 String sequenceNumber = record.getSequenceNumber();
2 long subSequenceNumber = ((UserRecord) record).getSubSequenceNumber();  // ... do other
       processing
3 checkpointer.checkpoint(sequenceNumber, subSequenceNumber);
```

The cast from `Record`to`UserRecord` always succeeds because the implementation always uses `UserRecord` under the hood. Unless there is a need to perform arithmetic on the sequence numbers, this approach is not recommended.

While processing KPL user records, the KCL writes the subsequence number into Amazon DynamoDB as an extra field for each row. Previous versions of the KCL used `AFTER_SEQUENCE_NUMBER` to fetch records when resuming checkpoints. The current KCL with KPL support uses `AT_SEQUENCE_NUMBER` instead. When the record at the checkpointed sequence number is retrieved, the checkpointed subsequence number is checked, and subrecords are dropped as appropriate (which may be all of them, if the last subrecord is the one checkpointed). Again, non-aggregated records can be thought of as aggregated records with a single subrecord, so the same algorithm works for both aggregated and non-aggregated records.

Using GetRecords Directly

You can also choose not to use the KCL but instead invoke the API operation `GetRecords` directly to retrieve Kinesis Data Streams records. To unpack these retrieved records into your original KPL user records, call one of the following static operations in `UserRecord.java`:

```
1 public static List<Record> deaggregate(List<Record> records)
2
3 public static List<UserRecord> deaggregate(List<UserRecord> records, BigInteger startingHashKey,
       BigInteger endingHashKey)
```

The first operation uses the default value 0 (zero) for `startingHashKey` and the default value 2^128 -1 for `endingHashKey`.

Each of these operations de-aggregates the given list of Kinesis Data Streams records into a list of KPL user records. Any KPL user records whose explicit hash key or partition key falls outside the range of the `startingHashKey` (inclusive) and the `endingHashKey` (inclusive) are discarded from the returned list of records.

Developing Amazon Kinesis Data Streams Producers Using the Amazon Kinesis Data Streams API with the AWS SDK for Java

You can develop producers using the Amazon Kinesis Data Streams API with the AWS SDK for Java. If you are new to Kinesis Data Streams, start by becoming familiar with the concepts and terminology presented in What Is Amazon Kinesis Data Streams? and Getting Started Using Amazon Kinesis Data Streams.

These examples discuss the Kinesis Data Streams API and use the AWS SDK for Java to add (put) data to a stream. However, for most use cases, you should prefer the Kinesis Data Streams KPL library. For more information, see Developing Amazon Kinesis Data Streams Producers Using the Kinesis Producer Library.

The Java example code in this chapter demonstrates how to perform basic Kinesis Data Streams API operations, and is divided up logically by operation type. These examples do not represent production-ready code, in that they do not check for all possible exceptions, or account for all possible security or performance considerations. Also, you can call the Kinesis Data Streams API using other programming languages. For more information about all available AWS SDKs, see Start Developing with Amazon Web Services.

Each task has prerequisites; for example, you cannot add data to a stream until you have created a stream, which requires you to create a client . For more information, see Managing Kinesis Data Streams Using Java.

Adding Data to a Stream

Once a stream is created, you can add data to it in the form of records. A record is a data structure that contains the data to be processed in the form of a data blob. After you store the data in the record, Kinesis Data Streams does not inspect, interpret, or change the data in any way. Each record also has an associated sequence number and partition key.

There are two different operations in the Kinesis Data Streams API that add data to a stream, http://docs. aws.amazon.com/kinesis/latest/APIReference/API_PutRecords.html and http://docs.aws.amazon.com/kinesis/latest/APIReference/API_PutRecord.html. The `PutRecords` operation sends multiple records to your stream per HTTP request, and the singular `PutRecord` operation sends records to your stream one at a time (a separate HTTP request is required for each record). You should prefer using `PutRecords` for most applications because it will achieve higher throughput per data producer. For more information about each of these operations, see the separate subsections below.

Topics

- Adding Multiple Records with PutRecords
- Adding a Single Record with PutRecord

Always keep in mind that, as your source application is adding data to the stream using the Kinesis Data Streams API, there are most likely one or more consumer applications that are simultaneously processing data off the stream. For information about how consumers get data using the Kinesis Data Streams API, see Getting Data from a Stream.

Important
Changing the Data Retention Period

Adding Multiple Records with PutRecords

The http://docs.aws.amazon.com/kinesis/latest/APIReference/API_PutRecords.html operation sends multiple records to Kinesis Data Streams in a single request. By using `PutRecords`, producers can achieve higher throughput when sending data to their Kinesis data stream. Each `PutRecords` request can support up to 500 records. Each record in the request can be as large as 1 MB, up to a limit of 5 MB for the entire request, including partition keys. As with the single `PutRecord` operation described below, `PutRecords` uses sequence numbers and partition keys. However, the `PutRecord` parameter `SequenceNumberForOrdering` is not included in a `PutRecords` call. The `PutRecords` operation attempts to process all records in the natural order of the request.

Each data record has a unique sequence number. The sequence number is assigned by Kinesis Data Streams after you call `client.putRecords` to add the data records to the stream. Sequence numbers for the same partition key generally increase over time; the longer the time period between `PutRecords` requests, the larger the sequence numbers become.

Note
Sequence numbers cannot be used as indexes to sets of data within the same stream. To logically separate sets of data, use partition keys or create a separate stream for each data set.

A `PutRecords` request can include records with different partition keys. The scope of the request is a stream; each request may include any combination of partition keys and records up to the request limits. Requests made with many different partition keys to streams with many different shards are generally faster than requests with a small number of partition keys to a small number of shards. The number of partition keys should be much larger than the number of shards to reduce latency and maximize throughput.

PutRecords Example

The following code creates 100 data records with sequential partition keys and puts them in a stream called `DataStream`.

```
1    AmazonKinesisClientBuilder clientBuilder = AmazonKinesisClientBuilder.standard();
2
3    clientBuilder.setRegion(regionName);
4    clientBuilder.setCredentials(credentialsProvider);
5    clientBuilder.setClientConfiguration(config);
6
7    AmazonKinesis kinesisClient = clientBuilder.build();
8
9    PutRecordsRequest putRecordsRequest  = new PutRecordsRequest();
10   putRecordsRequest.setStreamName(streamName);
11   List <PutRecordsRequestEntry> putRecordsRequestEntryList  = new ArrayList<>();
12   for (int i = 0; i < 100; i++) {
13       PutRecordsRequestEntry putRecordsRequestEntry  = new PutRecordsRequestEntry();
14       putRecordsRequestEntry.setData(ByteBuffer.wrap(String.valueOf(i).getBytes()));
15       putRecordsRequestEntry.setPartitionKey(String.format("partitionKey-%d", i));
16       putRecordsRequestEntryList.add(putRecordsRequestEntry);
17   }
18
19   putRecordsRequest.setRecords(putRecordsRequestEntryList);
20   PutRecordsResult putRecordsResult  = kinesisClient.putRecords(putRecordsRequest);
21   System.out.println("Put Result" + putRecordsResult);
```

The `PutRecords` response includes an array of response `Records`. Each record in the response array directly correlates with a record in the request array using natural ordering, from the top to the bottom of the request and response. The response `Records` array always includes the same number of records as the request array.

Handling failures when using PutRecords

By default, failure of individual records within a request does not stop the processing of subsequent records in a `PutRecords` request. This means that a response `Records` array includes both successfully and unsuccessfully processed records. You must detect unsuccessfully processed records and include them in a subsequent call.

Successful records include `SequenceNumber` and `ShardID` values, and unsuccessful records include `ErrorCode` and `ErrorMessage` values. The `ErrorCode` parameter reflects the type of error and can be one of the following values: `ProvisionedThroughputExceededException` or `InternalFailure`. `ErrorMessage` provides more detailed information about the `ProvisionedThroughputExceededException` exception including the account ID, stream name, and shard ID of the record that was throttled. The example below has three records in a `PutRecords` request. The second record fails and is reflected in the response.

Example PutRecords Request Syntax

```
1  {
2      "Records": [
3          {
4          "Data": "XzxkYXRhPl8w",
5          "PartitionKey": "partitionKey1"
6          },
7          {
8          "Data": "AbceddeRFfg12asd",
9          "PartitionKey": "partitionKey1"
10         },
11         {
12         "Data": "KFpcd98*7nd1",
13         "PartitionKey": "partitionKey3"
14         }
15     ],
16     "StreamName": "myStream"
17 }
```

Example PutRecords Response Syntax

```
1  {
2      ""FailedRecordCount: 1,
3      "Records": [
4          {
5          "SequenceNumber": "21269319989900637946712965403778482371",
6          "ShardId": "shardId-000000000001"
7
8          },
9          {"
10         ErrorCode"":"ProvisionedThroughputExceededException,"
11         ErrorMessage": "Rate exceeded for shard shardId-000000000001 in stream exampleStreamName
                under account 111111111111."
12
13         },
14         {
15         "SequenceNumber": "21269319989999637946712965403778482985",
16         "ShardId": "shardId-000000000002"
17         }
18     ]
19 }
```

Records that were unsuccessfully processed can be included in subsequent `PutRecords` requests. First, check the `FailedRecordCount` parameter in the `putRecordsResult` to confirm if there are failed records in the request. If so, each `putRecordsEntry` that has an `ErrorCode` that is not `null` should be added to a subsequent request. For an example of this type of handler, refer to the following code.

Example PutRecords failure handler

```
1 PutRecordsRequest putRecordsRequest = new PutRecordsRequest();
2 putRecordsRequest.setStreamName(myStreamName);
```

```java
3  List<PutRecordsRequestEntry> putRecordsRequestEntryList = new ArrayList<>();
4  for (int j = 0; j < 100; j++) {
5      PutRecordsRequestEntry putRecordsRequestEntry = new PutRecordsRequestEntry();
6      putRecordsRequestEntry.setData(ByteBuffer.wrap(String.valueOf(j).getBytes()));
7      putRecordsRequestEntry.setPartitionKey(String.format("partitionKey-%d", j));
8      putRecordsRequestEntryList.add(putRecordsRequestEntry);
9  }
10
11 putRecordsRequest.setRecords(putRecordsRequestEntryList);
12 PutRecordsResult putRecordsResult = amazonKinesisClient.putRecords(putRecordsRequest);
13
14 while (putRecordsResult.getFailedRecordCount() > 0) {
15     final List<PutRecordsRequestEntry> failedRecordsList = new ArrayList<>();
16     final List<PutRecordsResultEntry> putRecordsResultEntryList = putRecordsResult.getRecords();
17     for (int i = 0; i < putRecordsResultEntryList.size(); i++) {
18         final PutRecordsRequestEntry putRecordRequestEntry = putRecordsRequestEntryList.get(i);
19         final PutRecordsResultEntry putRecordsResultEntry = putRecordsResultEntryList.get(i);
20         if (putRecordsResultEntry.getErrorCode() != null) {
21             failedRecordsList.add(putRecordRequestEntry);
22         }
23     }
24     putRecordsRequestEntryList = failedRecordsList;
25     putRecordsRequest.setRecords(putRecordsRequestEntryList);
26     putRecordsResult = amazonKinesisClient.putRecords(putRecordsRequest);
27 }
```

Adding a Single Record with PutRecord

Each call to http://docs.aws.amazon.com/kinesis/latest/APIReference/API_PutRecord.html operates on a single record. Prefer the `PutRecords` operation described in Adding Multiple Records with PutRecords unless your application specifically needs to always send single records per request, or some other reason `PutRecords` can't be used.

Each data record has a unique sequence number. The sequence number is assigned by Kinesis Data Streams after you call `client.putRecord` to add the data record to the stream. Sequence numbers for the same partition key generally increase over time; the longer the time period between `PutRecord` requests, the larger the sequence numbers become.

When puts occur in quick succession, the returned sequence numbers are not guaranteed to increase because the put operations appear essentially as simultaneous to Kinesis Data Streams. To guarantee strictly increasing sequence numbers for the same partition key, use the `SequenceNumberForOrdering` parameter, as shown in the PutRecord Example code sample.

Whether or not you use `SequenceNumberForOrdering`, records that Kinesis Data Streams receives through a `GetRecords` call are strictly ordered by sequence number.

Note
Sequence numbers cannot be used as indexes to sets of data within the same stream. To logically separate sets of data, use partition keys or create a separate stream for each data set.

A partition key is used to group data within the stream. A data record is assigned to a shard within the stream based on its partition key. Specifically, Kinesis Data Streams uses the partition key as input to a hash function that maps the partition key (and associated data) to a specific shard.

As a result of this hashing mechanism, all data records with the same partition key map to the same shard within the stream. However, if the number of partition keys exceeds the number of shards, some shards necessarily contain records with different partition keys. From a design standpoint, to ensure that all your shards are well utilized, the number of shards (specified by the `setShardCount` method of `CreateStreamRequest`) should be substantially less than the number of unique partition keys, and the amount of data flowing to a single partition key should be substantially less than the capacity of the shard.

PutRecord Example

The following code creates ten data records, distributed across two partition keys, and puts them in a stream called `myStreamName`.

```
1  for (int j = 0; j < 10; j++)
2  {
3    PutRecordRequest putRecordRequest = new PutRecordRequest();
4    putRecordRequest.setStreamName( myStreamName );
5    putRecordRequest.setData(ByteBuffer.wrap( String.format( "testData-%d", j ).getBytes() ));
6    putRecordRequest.setPartitionKey( String.format( "partitionKey-%d", j/5 ));
7    putRecordRequest.setSequenceNumberForOrdering( sequenceNumberOfPreviousRecord );
8    PutRecordResult putRecordResult = client.putRecord( putRecordRequest );
9    sequenceNumberOfPreviousRecord = putRecordResult.getSequenceNumber();
10 }
```

The preceding code sample uses `setSequenceNumberForOrdering` to guarantee strictly increasing ordering within each partition key. To use this parameter effectively, set the `SequenceNumberForOrdering` of the current record (record *n*) to the sequence number of the preceding record (record *n-1*). To get the sequence number of a record that has been added to the stream, call `getSequenceNumber` on the result of `putRecord`.

The `SequenceNumberForOrdering` parameter ensures strictly increasing sequence numbers for the same partition key, when the same client calls `PutRecord`. `SequenceNumberForOrdering` does not provide ordering guarantees across records that are added from multiple concurrent applications, or across multiple partition keys.

Writing to Amazon Kinesis Data Streams Using Kinesis Agent

Kinesis Agent is a stand-alone Java software application that offers an easy way to collect and send data to Kinesis Data Streams. The agent continuously monitors a set of files and sends new data to your stream. The agent handles file rotation, checkpointing, and retry upon failures. It delivers all of your data in a reliable, timely, and simple manner. It also emits Amazon CloudWatch metrics to help you better monitor and troubleshoot the streaming process.

By default, records are parsed from each file based on the newline ('\n') character. However, the agent can also be configured to parse multi-line records (see Agent Configuration Settings).

You can install the agent on Linux-based server environments such as web servers, log servers, and database servers. After installing the agent, configure it by specifying the files to monitor and the stream for the data. After the agent is configured, it durably collects data from the files and reliably sends it to the stream.

Topics

- Prerequisites
- Download and Install the Agent
- Configure and Start the Agent
- Agent Configuration Settings
- Monitor Multiple File Directories and Write to Multiple Streams
- Use the Agent to Pre-process Data
- Agent CLI Commands

Prerequisites

- Your operating system must be either Amazon Linux AMI with version 2015.09 or later, or Red Hat Enterprise Linux version 7 or later.
- If you are using Amazon EC2 to run your agent, launch your EC2 instance.
- Manage your AWS credentials using one of the following methods:
  - Specify an IAM role when you launch your EC2 instance.
  - Specify AWS credentials when you configure the agent (see awsAccessKeyId and awsSecretAccessKey).
  - Edit /etc/sysconfig/aws-kinesis-agent to specify your region and AWS access keys.
  - If your EC2 instance is in a different AWS account, create an IAM role to provide access to the Kinesis Data Streams service, and specify that role when you configure the agent (see assumeRoleARN and assumeRoleExternalId). Use one of the previous methods to specify the AWS credentials of a user in the other account who has permission to assume this role.
- The IAM role or AWS credentials that you specify must have permission to perform the Kinesis Data Streams PutRecords operation for the agent to send data to your stream. If you enable CloudWatch monitoring for the agent, permission to perform the CloudWatch PutMetricData operation is also needed. For more information, see Controlling Access to Amazon Kinesis Data Streams Resources Using IAM, Monitoring Kinesis Data Streams Agent Health with Amazon CloudWatch, and CloudWatch Access Control.

Download and Install the Agent

First, connect to your instance. For more information, see Connect to Your Instance in the *Amazon EC2 User Guide for Linux Instances*. If you have trouble connecting, see Troubleshooting Connecting to Your Instance in the *Amazon EC2 User Guide for Linux Instances*.

To set up the agent using the Amazon Linux AMI
Use the following command to download and install the agent:

```
1  sudo yum install -y aws-kinesis-agent
```

To set up the agent using Red Hat Enterprise Linux

Use the following command to download and install the agent:

```
1 sudo yum install -y https://s3.amazonaws.com/streaming-data-agent/aws-kinesis-agent-latest.amzn1
    .noarch.rpm
```

To set up the agent using GitHub

1. Download the agent from awlabs/amazon-kinesis-agent.

2. Install the agent by navigating to the download directory and running the following command:

```
1 sudo ./setup --install
```

Configure and Start the Agent

To configure and start the agent

1. Open and edit the configuration file (as superuser if using default file access permissions): /etc/aws-kinesis/agent.json

   In this configuration file, specify the files ("filePattern") from which the agent collects data, and the name of the stream ("kinesisStream") to which the agent sends data. Note that the file name is a pattern, and the agent recognizes file rotations. You can rotate files or create new files no more than once per second. The agent uses the file creation timestamp to determine which files to track and tail into your stream; creating new files or rotating files more frequently than once per second does not allow the agent to differentiate properly between them.

```
1 {
2    "flows": [
3        {
4            "filePattern": "/tmp/app.log*",
5            "kinesisStream": "yourkinesisstream"
6        }
7    ]
8 }
```

2. Start the agent manually:

```
1 sudo service aws-kinesis-agent start
```

3. (Optional) Configure the agent to start on system startup:

```
1 sudo chkconfig aws-kinesis-agent on
```

The agent is now running as a system service in the background. It continuously monitors the specified files and sends data to the specified stream. Agent activity is logged in /var/log/aws-kinesis-agent/aws-kinesis-agent.log.

Agent Configuration Settings

The agent supports the two mandatory configuration settings, filePattern and kinesisStream, plus optional configuration settings for additional features. You can specify both mandatory and optional configuration in /etc/aws-kinesis/agent.json.

Whenever you change the configuration file, you must stop and start the agent, using the following commands:

```
1 sudo service aws-kinesis-agent stop
2 sudo service aws-kinesis-agent start
```

Alternatively, you could use the following command:

```
1 sudo service aws-kinesis-agent restart
```

The following are the general configuration settings.

Configuration Setting	Description
assumeRoleARN	The ARN of the role to be assumed by the user. For more information, see Delegate Access Across AWS Accounts Using IAM Roles in the *IAM User Guide*.
assumeRoleExternalId	An optional identifier that determines who can assume the role. For more information, see How to Use an External ID in the *IAM User Guide*.
awsAccessKeyId	AWS access key ID that overrides the default credentials. This setting takes precedence over all other credential providers.
awsSecretAccessKey	AWS secret key that overrides the default credentials. This setting takes precedence over all other credential providers.
cloudwatch.emitMetrics	Enables the agent to emit metrics to Cloud-Watch if set (true). Default: true
cloudwatch.endpoint	The regional endpoint for CloudWatch. Default: `monitoring.us-east-1.amazonaws.com`
kinesis.endpoint	The regional endpoint for Kinesis Data Streams. Default: `kinesis.us-east-1.amazonaws.com`

The following are the flow configuration settings.

Configuration Setting	Description
dataProcessingOptions	The list of processing options applied to each parsed record before it is sent to the stream. The processing options are performed in the specified order. For more information, see Use the Agent to Pre-process Data.
kinesisStream	[Required] The name of the stream.
filePattern	[Required] A glob for the files that must be monitored by the agent. Any file that matches this pattern is picked up by the agent automatically and monitored. For all files matching this pattern, read permission must be granted to `aws-kinesis-agent-user`. For the directory containing the files, read and execute permissions must be granted to `aws-kinesis-agent-user`.

Configuration Setting	Description
initialPosition	The initial position from which the file started to be parsed. Valid values are `START_OF_FILE` and `END_OF_FILE`. Default: `END_OF_FILE`
maxBufferAgeMillis	The maximum time, in milliseconds, for which the agent buffers data before sending it to the stream. Value range: 1,000 to 900,000 (1 second to 15 minutes) Default: 60,000 (1 minute)
maxBufferSizeBytes	The maximum size, in bytes, for which the agent buffers data before sending it to the stream. Value range: 1 to 4,194,304 (4 MB) Default: 4,194,304 (4 MB)
maxBufferSizeRecords	The maximum number of records for which the agent buffers data before sending it to the stream. Value range: 1 to 500 Default: 500
minTimeBetweenFilePollsMillis	The time interval, in milliseconds, at which the agent polls and parses the monitored files for new data. Value range: 1 or more Default: 100
multiLineStartPattern	The pattern for identifying the start of a record. A record is made of a line that matches the pattern and any following lines that don't match the pattern. The valid values are regular expressions. By default, each new line in the log files is parsed as one record.
partitionKeyOption	The method for generating the partition key. Valid values are `RANDOM` (randomonly generated integer) and `DETERMINISTIC` (a hash value computed from the data). Default: `RANDOM`
skipHeaderLines	The number of lines for the agent to skip parsing at the beginning of monitored files. Value range: 0 or more Default: 0 (zero)
truncatedRecordTerminator	The string that the agent uses to truncate a parsed record when the record size exceeds the Kinesis Data Streams record size limit. (1,000 KB) Default: `'\n'` (newline)

Monitor Multiple File Directories and Write to Multiple Streams

By specifying multiple flow configuration settings, you can configure the agent to monitor multiple file directories and send data to multiple streams. In the following configuration example, the agent monitors two file directories and sends data to an Kinesis stream and a Kinesis Firehose delivery stream respectively. Note that you can specify different endpoints for Kinesis Data Streams and Kinesis Firehose so that your Kinesis stream and Kinesis Firehose delivery stream don't need to be in the same region.

```
1 {
2     "cloudwatch.emitMetrics": true,
3     "kinesis.endpoint": "https://your/kinesis/endpoint",
4     "firehose.endpoint": "https://your/firehose/endpoint",
5     "flows": [
```

```
 6          {
 7              "filePattern": "/tmp/app1.log*",
 8              "kinesisStream": "yourkinesisstream"
 9          },
10          {
11              "filePattern": "/tmp/app2.log*",
12              "deliveryStream": "yourfirehosedeliverystream"
13          }
14      ]
15 }
```

For more detailed information about using the agent with Kinesis Firehose, see Writing to Amazon Kinesis Data Firehose with Kinesis Agent.

Use the Agent to Pre-process Data

The agent can pre-process the records parsed from monitored files before sending them to your stream. You can enable this feature by adding the `dataProcessingOptions` configuration setting to your file flow. One or more processing options can be added and they will be performed in the specified order.

The agent supports the following processing options listed. Because the agent is open-source, you can further develop and extend its processing options. You can download the agent from Kinesis Agent.Processing Options

SINGLELINE
Converts a multi-line record to a single line record by removing newline characters, leading spaces, and trailing spaces.

```
1 {
2     "optionName": "SINGLELINE"
3 }
```

CSVTOJSON
Converts a record from delimiter separated format to JSON format.

```
1 {
2     "optionName": "CSVTOJSON",
3     "customFieldNames": [ "field1", "field2", ... ],
4     "delimiter": "yourdelimiter"
5 }
```

customFieldNames
[Required] The field names used as keys in each JSON key value pair. For example, if you specify ["f1", "f2"], the record "v1, v2" will be converted to {"f1":"v1","f2":"v2"}.
delimiter
The string used as the delimiter in the record. The default is a comma (,).

LOGTOJSON
Converts a record from a log format to JSON format. The supported log formats are Apache Common Log, Apache Combined Log, Apache Error Log, and RFC3164 Syslog.

```
1 {
2     "optionName": "LOGTOJSON",
3     "logFormat": "logformat",
4     "matchPattern": "yourregexpattern",
5     "customFieldNames": [ "field1", "field2", … ]
6 }
```

80

```
logFormat
```
[Required] The log entry format. The following are possible values:

- `COMMONAPACHELOG` — The Apache Common Log format. Each log entry has the following pattern by default: "%{host} %{ident} %{authuser} [%{datetime}] \"%{request}\" %{response} %{bytes}".
- `COMBINEDAPACHELOG` — The Apache Combined Log format. Each log entry has the following pattern by default: "%{host} %{ident} %{authuser} [%{datetime}] \"%{request}\" %{response} %{bytes} } %{referrer} %{agent}".
- `APACHEERRORLOG` — The Apache Error Log format. Each log entry has the following pattern by default: "[%{timestamp}] [%{module}:%{severity}] [pid %{processid}:tid %{threadid}] [client : %{client}] %{message}".
- `SYSLOG` — The RFC3164 Syslog format. Each log entry has the following pattern by default: "%{timestamp} %{hostname} %{program}[%{processid}]: %{message}".

```
matchPattern
```
The regular expression pattern used to extract values from log entries. This setting is used if your log entry is not in one of the predefined log formats. If this setting is used, you must also specify `customFieldNames`.

```
customFieldNames
```
The custom field names used as keys in each JSON key value pair. You can use this setting to define field names for values extracted from `matchPattern`, or override the default field names of predefined log formats.

Example : LOGTOJSON Configuration Here is one example of a `LOGTOJSON` configuration for an Apache Common Log entry converted to JSON format:

```
1 {
2     "optionName": "LOGTOJSON",
3     "logFormat": "COMMONAPACHELOG"
4 }
```

Before conversion:

```
1 64.242.88.10 - - [07/Mar/2004:16:10:02 -0800] "GET /mailman/listinfo/hsdivision HTTP/1.1" 200
    6291
```

After conversion:

```
1 {"host":"64.242.88.10","ident":null,"authuser":null,"datetime":"07/Mar/2004:16:10:02 -0800","
    request":"GET /mailman/listinfo/hsdivision HTTP/1.1","response":"200","bytes":"6291"}
```

Example : LOGTOJSON Configuration With Custom Fields Here is another example `LOGTOJSON` configuration:

```
1 {
2     "optionName": "LOGTOJSON",
3     "logFormat": "COMMONAPACHELOG",
4     "customFieldNames": ["f1", "f2", "f3", "f4", "f5", "f6", "f7"]
5 }
```

With this configuration setting, the same Apache Common Log entry from the previous example is converted to JSON format as follows:

```
1 {"f1":"64.242.88.10","f2":null,"f3":null,"f4":"07/Mar/2004:16:10:02 -0800","f5":"GET /mailman/
    listinfo/hsdivision HTTP/1.1","f6":"200","f7":"6291"}
```

Example : Convert Apache Common Log Entry The following flow configuration converts an Apache Common Log entry to a single line record in JSON format:

```
1 {
2     "flows": [
```

```
 3          {
 4              "filePattern": "/tmp/app.log*",
 5              "kinesisStream": "my-stream",
 6              "dataProcessingOptions": [
 7                  {
 8                      "optionName": "LOGTOJSON",
 9                      "logFormat": "COMMONAPACHELOG"
10                  }
11              ]
12          }
13      ]
14 }
```

Example : Convert Multi-Line Records The following flow configuration parses multi-line records whose first line starts with "[SEQUENCE=". Each record is first converted to a single line record. Then, values are extracted from the record based on a tab delimiter. Extracted values are mapped to specified `customFieldNames` values to form a single-line record in JSON format.

```
 1 {
 2      "flows": [
 3          {
 4              "filePattern": "/tmp/app.log*",
 5              "kinesisStream": "my-stream",
 6              "multiLineStartPattern": "\\[SEQUENCE=",
 7              "dataProcessingOptions": [
 8                  {
 9                      "optionName": "SINGLELINE"
10                  },
11                  {
12                      "optionName": "CSVTOJSON",
13                      "customFieldNames": [ "field1", "field2", "field3" ],
14                      "delimiter": "\\t"
15                  }
16              ]
17          }
18      ]
19 }
```

Example : LOGTOJSON Configuration with Match Pattern Here is one example of a LOGTOJSON configuration for an Apache Common Log entry converted to JSON format, with the last field (bytes) omitted:

```
 1 {
 2      "optionName": "LOGTOJSON",
 3      "logFormat": "COMMONAPACHELOG",
 4      "matchPattern": "^([\\d.]+) (\\S+) (\\S+) \\[([\\w:/]+\\s[+\\-]\\d{4})\\] \"(.+?)\" (\\d{3})
            ",
 5      "customFieldNames": ["host", "ident", "authuser", "datetime", "request", "response"]
 6 }
```

Before conversion:

```
 1 123.45.67.89 - - [27/Oct/2000:09:27:09 -0400] "GET /java/javaResources.html HTTP/1.0" 200
```

After conversion:

```
 1 {"host":"123.45.67.89","ident":null,"authuser":null,"datetime":"27/Oct/2000:09:27:09 -0400","
      request":"GET /java/javaResources.html HTTP/1.0","response":"200"}
```

Agent CLI Commands

Automatically start the agent on system startup:

```
1 sudo chkconfig aws-kinesis-agent on
```

Check the status of the agent:

```
1 sudo service aws-kinesis-agent status
```

Stop the agent:

```
1 sudo service aws-kinesis-agent stop
```

Read the agent's log file from this location:

```
1 /var/log/aws-kinesis-agent/aws-kinesis-agent.log
```

Uninstall the agent:

```
1 sudo yum remove aws-kinesis-agent
```

Troubleshooting Amazon Kinesis Data Streams Producers

Topics

- Producer Application is Writing at a Slower Rate Than Expected
- Unauthorized KMS master key permission error

Producer Application is Writing at a Slower Rate Than Expected

Topics

- Service Limits Exceeded
- Producer Optimization

Service Limits Exceeded

To find out if service limits are being exceeded, check to see if your producer is throwing throughput exceptions from the service, and validate what API operations are being throttled. Keep in mind that there are different limits based on the call, see Amazon Kinesis Data Streams Limits. For example, in addition to the shard-level limits for writes and reads that are most commonly known, there are the following stream-level limits:

- CreateStream
- DeleteStream
- ListStreams
- GetShardIterator
- MergeShards
- DescribeStream
- DescribeStreamSummary

The operations `CreateStream`, `DeleteStream`, `ListStreams`, `GetShardIterator`, and `MergeShards` are limited to 5 calls per second. The `DescribeStream` operation is limited to 10 calls per second. The `DescribeStreamSummary` operation is limited to 20 calls per second.

If these calls aren't the issue, make sure you've selected a partition key that allows you to distribute *put* operations evenly across all shards, and that you don't have a particular partition key that's bumping into the service limits when the rest are not. This requires that you measure peak throughput and take into account the number of shards in your stream. For more information about managing streams, see Managing Kinesis Data Streams Using Java.

Tip

Remember to round up to the nearest kilobyte for throughput throttling calculations when using the single-record operation PutRecord, while the multi-record operation PutRecords rounds on the cumulative sum of the records in each call. For example, a `PutRecords` request with 600 records that are 1.1 KB in size will not get throttled.

Producer Optimization

Before you begin optimizing your producer, there are some key tasks to be completed. First, identify your desired peak throughput in terms of record size and records per second. Next, rule out stream capacity as the limiting factor (Service Limits Exceeded). If you've ruled out stream capacity, use the following troubleshooting tips and optimization guidelines for the two common types of producers.

Large Producer

A large producer is usually running from an on-premises server or Amazon EC2 instance. Customers who need higher throughput from a large producer typically care about per-record latency. Strategies for dealing with latency include the following: If the customer can micro-batch/buffer records, use the Kinesis Producer Library (which has advanced aggregation logic), the multi-record operation PutRecords, or aggregate records into a larger file before using the single-record operation PutRecord. If you are unable to batch/buffer, use multiple threads to write to the Kinesis Data Streams service at the same time. The AWS SDK for Java and other SDKs include async clients that can do this with very little code.

Small Producer

A small producer is usually a mobile app, IoT device, or web client. If it's a mobile app, we recommend using the `PutRecords` operation or the Kinesis Recorder in the AWS Mobile SDKs. For more information, see AWS Mobile SDK for Android Getting Started Guide and AWS Mobile SDK for iOS Getting Started Guide. Mobile apps must handle intermittent connections inherently and need some sort of batch put, such as `PutRecords`. If you are unable to batch for some reason, see the Large Producer information above. If your producer is a browser, the amount of data being generated is typically very small. However, you are putting the *put* operations on the critical path of the application, which we don't recommend.

Unauthorized KMS master key permission error

This error occurs when a producer application writes to an encrypted stream without permissions on the KMS master key. To assign permissions to an application to access a KMS key, see Using Key Policies in AWS KMS and Using IAM Policies with AWS KMS.

Advanced Topics for Amazon Kinesis Data Streams Producers

This section discusses how to optimize your Amazon Kinesis Data Streams producers.

Topics

- KPL Retries and Rate Limiting
- Considerations When Using KPL Aggregation

KPL Retries and Rate Limiting

When you add KPL user records using the KPL `addUserRecord()` operation, a record is given a timestamp and added to a buffer with a deadline set by the `RecordMaxBufferedTime` configuration parameter. This timestamp/deadline combination sets the buffer priority. Records are flushed from the buffer based on the following criteria:

- Buffer priority
- Aggregation configuration
- Collection configuration

The aggregation and collection configuration parameters affecting buffer behavior are as follows:

- `AggregationMaxCount`
- `AggregationMaxSize`
- `CollectionMaxCount`
- `CollectionMaxSize`

Records flushed are then sent to your Kinesis data stream as Amazon Kinesis Data Streams records using a call to the Kinesis Data Streams API operation `PutRecords`. The `PutRecords` operation sends requests to your stream that occasionally exhibit full or partial failures. Records that fail are automatically added back to the KPL buffer. The new deadline is set based on the minimum of these two values:

- Half the current `RecordMaxBufferedTime` configuration
- The record's time-to-live value

This strategy allows retried KPL user records to be included in subsequent Kinesis Data Streams API calls, to improve throughput and reduce complexity while enforcing the Kinesis Data Streams record's time-to-live value. There is no backoff algorithm, making this a relatively aggressive retry strategy. Spamming due to excessive retries is prevented by rate limiting, discussed in the next section.

Rate Limiting

The KPL includes a rate limiting feature, which limits per-shard throughput sent from a single producer. Rate limiting is implemented using a token bucket algorithm with separate buckets for both Kinesis Data Streams records and bytes. Each successful write to an Kinesis data stream adds a token (or multiple tokens) to each bucket, up to a certain threshold. This threshold is configurable but by default is set 50% higher than the actual shard limit, to allow shard saturation from a single producer.

You can lower this limit to reduce spamming due to excessive retries. However, the best practice is for each producer is to retry for maximum throughput aggressively and to handle any resulting throttling determined as excessive by expanding the capacity of the stream and implementing an appropriate partition key strategy.

Considerations When Using KPL Aggregation

While the sequence number scheme of the resulting Amazon Kinesis Data Streams records remains the same, aggregation causes the indexing of KPL user records contained within an aggregated Kinesis Data Streams record to start at 0 (zero); however, as long as you do not rely on sequence numbers to uniquely identify your KPL user records, your code can ignore this, as the aggregation (of your KPL user records into a Kinesis Data Streams record) and subsequent de-aggregation (of a Kinesis Data Streams record into your KPL user records) automatically takes care of this for you. This applies whether your consumer is using the KCL or the AWS SDK. To use this aggregation functionality, you'll need to pull the Java part of the KPL into your build if your consumer is written using the API provided in the AWS SDK.

If you intend to use sequence numbers as unique identifiers for your KPL user records, we recommend that you use the contract-abiding `public int hashCode()` and `public boolean equals(Object obj)` operations provided in `Record` and `UserRecord` to enable the comparison of your KPL user records. Additionally, if you wish to examine the subsequence number of your KPL user record, you can cast it to a `UserRecord` instance and retrieve its subsequence number.

For more information, see Consumer De-aggregation.

Reading Data From Amazon Kinesis Data Streams

A *consumer* is an application that reads and processes data from Amazon Kinesis Data Streams. You can build consumers for Kinesis Data Streams. If you are new to Kinesis Data Streams, start by becoming familiar with the concepts and terminology presented in What Is Amazon Kinesis Data Streams? and Getting Started Using Amazon Kinesis Data Streams.

Topics

- Developing Amazon Kinesis Data Streams Consumers Using the Kinesis Client Library
- Developing Amazon Kinesis Data Streams Consumers Using the Amazon Kinesis Data Streams API with the AWS SDK for Java
- Troubleshooting Amazon Kinesis Data Streams Consumers
- Advanced Topics for Amazon Kinesis Data Streams Consumers

Developing Amazon Kinesis Data Streams Consumers Using the Kinesis Client Library

You can develop a consumer application for Amazon Kinesis Data Streams using the Kinesis Client Library (KCL). Although you can use the Kinesis Data Streams API to get data from a Kinesis data stream, we recommend using the design patterns and code for consumer applications provided by the KCL.

You can monitor the KCL with Amazon CloudWatch. For more information, see Monitoring the Kinesis Client Library with Amazon CloudWatch.

Topics

- Kinesis Client Library
- Role of the KCL
- Developing a Kinesis Client Library Consumer in Java
- Developing a Kinesis Client Library Consumer in Node.js
- Developing a Kinesis Client Library Consumer in .NET
- Developing a Kinesis Client Library Consumer in Python
- Developing a Kinesis Client Library Consumer in Ruby

Kinesis Client Library

The Kinesis Client Library (KCL) helps you consume and process data from a Kinesis data stream. This type of application is also referred to as a *consumer*. The KCL takes care of many of the complex tasks associated with distributed computing, such as load-balancing across multiple instances, responding to instance failures, checkpointing processed records, and reacting to resharding. The KCL enables you to focus on writing record processing logic.

Note that the KCL is different from the Kinesis Data Streams API that is available in the AWS SDKs. The Kinesis Data Streams API helps you manage many aspects of Kinesis Data Streams (including creating streams, resharding, and putting and getting records), while the KCL provides a layer of abstraction specifically for processing data in a consumer role. For information about the Kinesis Data Streams API, see the Amazon Kinesis API Reference.

The KCL is a Java library; support for languages other than Java is provided using a multi-language interface called the *MultiLangDaemon*. This daemon is Java-based and runs in the background when you are using a KCL language other than Java. For example, if you install the KCL for Python and write your consumer app entirely in Python, you still need Java installed on your system because of the MultiLangDaemon. Further, MultiLangDaemon has some default settings you may need to customize for your use case, for example the AWS region it connects to. For more information about the MultiLangDaemon, go to the KCL MultiLangDaemon project page on GitHub.

At run time, a KCL application instantiates a worker with configuration information, and then uses a record processor to process the data received from a Kinesis data stream. You can run a KCL application on any number of instances. Multiple instances of the same application coordinate on failures and load-balance dynamically. You can also have multiple KCL applications working on the same stream, subject to throughput limits.

Role of the KCL

The KCL acts as an intermediary between your record processing logic and Kinesis Data Streams.

When you start a KCL application, it calls the KCL to instantiate a *worker*. This call provides the KCL with configuration information for the application, such as the stream name and AWS credentials.

The KCL performs the following tasks:

- Connects to the stream
- Enumerates the shards
- Coordinates shard associations with other workers (if any)
- Instantiates a record processor for every shard it manages
- Pulls data records from the stream
- Pushes the records to the corresponding record processor
- Checkpoints processed records
- Balances shard-worker associations when the worker instance count changes
- Balances shard-worker associations when shards are split or merged

Developing a Kinesis Client Library Consumer in Java

You can use the Kinesis Client Library (KCL) to build applications that process data from your Kinesis data streams. The Kinesis Client Library is available in multiple languages. This topic discusses Java. To view the javadoc reference, go to the AWS javadoc topic for Class AmazonKinesisClient.

To download the Java KCL from GitHub, go to Kinesis Client Library (Java). To locate the Java KCL on Maven, go to the KCL search results page. To download sample code for a Java KCL consumer application from GitHub, go to the KCL for Java sample project page on GitHub.

The sample application uses Apache Commons Logging. You can change the logging configuration in the static `configure` method defined in the file `AmazonKinesisApplicationSample.java`. For more information about how to use Apache Commons Logging with Log4j and AWS Java applications, see Logging with Log4j in the *AWS SDK for Java Developer Guide*.

You must complete the following tasks when implementing a KCL consumer application in Java:

Topics

- Implement the IRecordProcessor Methods
- Implement a Class Factory for the IRecordProcessor Interface
- Create a Worker
- Modify the Configuration Properties
- Migrating to Version 2 of the Record Processor Interface

Implement the IRecordProcessor Methods

The KCL currently supports two versions of the `IRecordProcessor` interface — the original interface available with the first version of the KCL, and version 2 available starting with KCL version 1.5.0. Both interfaces are fully supported; your choice depends on your specific scenario requirements. Refer to your locally-built Javadocs or the source code to see all the differences. The following sections outline the minimal implementation for getting started.

Topics

- Original Interface (Version 1)
- Updated Interface (Version 2)

Original Interface (Version 1)

The original `IRecordProcessor` interface (package `com.amazonaws.services.kinesis.clientlibrary.interfaces`) exposes the following record processor methods that your consumer must implement. The sample provides implementations that you can use as a starting point (see `AmazonKinesisApplicationSampleRecordProcessor.java`).

```
1 public void initialize(String shardId)
2 public void processRecords(List<Record> records, IRecordProcessorCheckpointer checkpointer)
3 public void shutdown(IRecordProcessorCheckpointer checkpointer, ShutdownReason reason)
```

initialize
The KCL calls the `initialize` method when the record processor is instantiated, passing a specific shard ID as a parameter. This record processor processes only this shard and typically, the reverse is also true (this shard is processed only by this record processor). However, your consumer should account for the possibility that a data record might be processed more than one time. Kinesis Data Streams has "at least once" semantics, meaning that every data record from a shard is processed at least one time by a worker in your consumer. For more information about cases in which a particular shard may be processed by more than one worker, see Resharding, Scaling, and Parallel Processing.

```
1 public void initialize(String shardId)
```

processRecords

The KCL calls the `processRecords` method, passing a list of data record from the shard specified by the `initialize(shardId)` method. The record processor processes the data in these records according to the semantics of the consumer. For example, the worker might perform a transformation on the data and then store the result in an Amazon S3 bucket.

```
1 public void processRecords(List<Record> records, IRecordProcessorCheckpointer checkpointer)
```

In addition to the data itself, the record also contains a sequence number and partition key. The worker can use these values when processing the data. For example, the worker could choose the S3 bucket in which to store the data based on the value of the partition key. The `Record` class exposes the following methods that provide access to the record's data, sequence number, and partition key.

```
1 record.getData()
2 record.getSequenceNumber()
3 record.getPartitionKey()
```

In the sample, the private method `processRecordsWithRetries` has code that shows how a worker can access the record's data, sequence number, and partition key.

Kinesis Data Streams requires the record processor to keep track of the records that have already been processed in a shard. The KCL takes care of this tracking for you by passing a checkpointer (`IRecordProcessorCheckpointer`) to `processRecords`. The record processor calls the `checkpoint` method on this interface to inform the KCL of how far it has progressed in processing the records in the shard. In the event that the worker fails, the KCL uses this information to restart the processing of the shard at the last known processed record.

In the case of a split or merge operation, the KCL won't start processing the new shards until the processors for the original shards have called `checkpoint` to signal that all processing on the original shards is complete.

If you don't pass a parameter, the KCL assumes that the call to `checkpoint` means that all records have been processed, up to the last record that was passed to the record processor. Therefore, the record processor should call `checkpoint` only after it has processed all the records in the list that was passed to it. Record processors do not need to call `checkpoint` on each call to `processRecords`. A processor could, for example, call `checkpoint` on every third call to `processRecords`. You can optionally specify the exact sequence number of a record as a parameter to `checkpoint`. In this case, the KCL assumes that all records have been processed up to that record only.

In the sample, the private method `checkpoint` shows how to call `IRecordProcessorCheckpointer.checkpoint` using the appropriate exception handling and retry logic.

The KCL relies on `processRecords` to handle any exceptions that arise from processing the data records. If an exception is thrown from `processRecords`, the KCL skips over the data records that were passed prior to the exception; that is, these records are not re-sent to the record processor that threw the exception or to any other record processor in the consumer.

shutdown

The KCL calls the `shutdown` method either when processing ends (the shutdown reason is TERMINATE) or the worker is no longer responding (the shutdown reason is ZOMBIE).

```
1 public void shutdown(IRecordProcessorCheckpointer checkpointer, ShutdownReason reason)
```

Processing ends when the record processor does not receive any further records from the shard, because either the shard was split or merged, or the stream was deleted.

The KCL also passes a `IRecordProcessorCheckpointer` interface to `shutdown`. If the shutdown reason is TERMINATE, the record processor should finish processing any data records, and then call the `checkpoint` method on this interface.

Updated Interface (Version 2)

The updated `IRecordProcessor` interface (package `com.amazonaws.services.kinesis.clientlibrary.`
`interfaces.v2`) exposes the following record processor methods that your consumer must implement:

```
1 void initialize(InitializationInput initializationInput)
2 void processRecords(ProcessRecordsInput processRecordsInput)
3 void shutdown(ShutdownInput shutdownInput)
```

All of the arguments from the original version of the interface are accessible through get methods on the container objects. For example, to retrieve the list of records in `processRecords()`, you can use `processRecordsInput.`
`getRecords()`.

As of version 2 of this interface (KCL 1.5.0 and later), the following new inputs are available in addition to the inputs provided by the original interface:

starting sequence number
In the `InitializationInput` object passed to the `initialize()` operation, the starting sequence number from which records would be provided to the record processor instance. This is the sequence number that was last checkpointed by the record processor instance previously processing the same shard. This is provided in case your application needs this information.

pending checkpoint sequence number
In the `InitializationInput` object passed to the `initialize()` operation, the pending checkpoint sequence number (if any) that could not be committed before the previous record processor instance stopped.

Implement a Class Factory for the IRecordProcessor Interface

You'll also need to implement a factory for the class that implements the record processor methods. When your consumer instantiates the worker, it passes a reference to this factory.

The sample implements the factory class in the file `AmazonKinesisApplicationSampleRecordProcessorFactory`
`.java` using the original record processor interface. If you want the class factory to create version 2 record processors, use the package name `com.amazonaws.services.kinesis.clientlibrary.interfaces.v2`.

```
1   public class SampleRecordProcessorFactory implements IRecordProcessorFactory {
2       /**
3        * Constructor.
4        */
5       public SampleRecordProcessorFactory() {
6           super();
7       }
8       /**
9        * {@inheritDoc}
10       */
11      @Override
12      public IRecordProcessor createProcessor() {
13          return new SampleRecordProcessor();
14      }
15  }
```

Create a Worker

As discussed in Implement the IRecordProcessor Methods, there are two versions of the KCL record processor interface to choose from, which affects how you would create a worker. The original record processor interface uses the following code structure to create a worker:

94

```
1 final KinesisClientLibConfiguration config = new KinesisClientLibConfiguration(...)
2 final IRecordProcessorFactory recordProcessorFactory = new RecordProcessorFactory();
3 final Worker worker = new Worker(recordProcessorFactory, config);
```

With version 2 of the record processor interface, you can use `Worker.Builder` to create a worker without needing to worry about which constructor to use and the order of the arguments. The updated record processor interface uses the following code structure to create a worker:

```
1 final KinesisClientLibConfiguration config = new KinesisClientLibConfiguration(...)
2 final IRecordProcessorFactory recordProcessorFactory = new RecordProcessorFactory();
3 final Worker worker = new Worker.Builder()
4     .recordProcessorFactory(recordProcessorFactory)
5     .config(config)
6     .build();
```

Modify the Configuration Properties

The sample provides default values for configuration properties. This configuration data for the worker is then consolidated in a `KinesisClientLibConfiguration` object. This object and a reference to the class factory for `IRecordProcessor` are passed in the call that instantiates the worker. You can override any of these properties with your own values using a Java properties file (see `AmazonKinesisApplicationSample.java`).

Application Name

The KCL requires an application name that is unique across your applications, and across DynamoDB tables in the same region. It uses the application name configuration value in the following ways:

- All workers associated with this application name are assumed to be working together on the same stream. These workers may be distributed on multiple instances. If you run an additional instance of the same application code, but with a different application name, the KCL treats the second instance as an entirely separate application that is also operating on the same stream.
- The KCL creates a DynamoDB table with the application name and uses the table to maintain state information (such as checkpoints and worker-shard mapping) for the application. Each application has its own DynamoDB table. For more information, see Tracking Amazon Kinesis Data Streams Application State.

Set Up Credentials

You must make your AWS credentials available to one of the credential providers in the default credential providers chain. For example, if you are running your consumer on an EC2 instance, we recommend that you launch the instance with an IAM role. AWS credentials that reflect the permissions associated with this IAM role are made available to applications on the instance through its instance metadata. This is the most secure way to manage credentials for a consumer running on an EC2 instance.

The sample application first attempts to retrieve IAM credentials from instance metadata:

```
1 credentialsProvider = new InstanceProfileCredentialsProvider();
```

If the sample application cannot obtain credentials from the instance metadata, it attempts to retrieve credentials from a properties file:

```
1 credentialsProvider = new ClasspathPropertiesFileCredentialsProvider();
```

For more information about instance metadata, see Instance Metadata in the *Amazon EC2 User Guide for Linux Instances.*

Use Worker ID for Multiple Instances

The sample initialization code creates an ID for the worker, `workerId`, using the name of the local computer and appending a globally unique identifier as shown in the following code snippet. This approach supports the scenario of multiple instances of the consumer application running on a single computer.

```
1 String workerId = InetAddress.getLocalHost().getCanonicalHostName() + ":" + UUID.randomUUID();
```

Migrating to Version 2 of the Record Processor Interface

If you would like to migrate code that uses the original interface, in addition to the steps described above, the following steps are required:

1. Change your record processor class to import the version 2 record processor interface:

```
1 import com.amazonaws.services.kinesis.clientlibrary.interfaces.v2.IRecordProcessor;
```

2. Change the references to inputs to use get methods on the container objects. For example, in the `shutdown()` operation, change "checkpointer" to "shutdownInput.getCheckpointer()".

3. Change your record processor factory class to import the version 2 record processor factory interface:

```
1 import com.amazonaws.services.kinesis.clientlibrary.interfaces.v2.IRecordProcessorFactory;
```

4. Change the construction of the worker to use `Worker.Builder`. For example:

```
1 final Worker worker = new Worker.Builder()
2     .recordProcessorFactory(recordProcessorFactory)
3     .config(config)
4     .build();
```

Developing a Kinesis Client Library Consumer in Node.js

You can use the Kinesis Client Library (KCL) to build applications that process data from your Kinesis data streams. The Kinesis Client Library is available in multiple languages. This topic discusses Node.js.

The KCL is a Java library; support for languages other than Java is provided using a multi-language interface called the *MultiLangDaemon*. This daemon is Java-based and runs in the background when you are using a KCL language other than Java. Therefore, if you install the KCL for Node.js and write your consumer app entirely in Node.js, you still need Java installed on your system because of the MultiLangDaemon. Further, MultiLangDaemon has some default settings you may need to customize for your use case, for example the AWS region it connects to. For more information about the MultiLangDaemon on GitHub, go to the KCL MultiLangDaemon project page.

To download the Node.js KCL from GitHub, go to Kinesis Client Library (Node.js).

Sample Code Downloads

There are two code samples available for KCL in Node.js:

- basic-sample

  Used in the following sections to illustrate the fundamentals of building a KCL consumer application in Node.js.

- click-stream-sample

  Slightly more advanced and uses a real-world scenario, after you have familiarized yourself with the basic sample code. This sample is not discussed here but has a README file with more information.

You must complete the following tasks when implementing a KCL consumer application in Node.js:

Topics

- Implement the Record Processor
- Modify the Configuration Properties

Implement the Record Processor

The simplest possible consumer using the KCL for Node.js must implement a `recordProcessor` function, which in turn contains the functions `initialize`, `processRecords`, and `shutdown`. The sample provides an implementation that you can use as a starting point (see `sample_kcl_app.js`).

```
1 function recordProcessor() {
2   // return an object that implements initialize, processRecords and shutdown functions.}
```

initialize
The KCL calls the `initialize` function when the record processor starts. This record processor processes only the shard ID passed as `initializeInput.shardId`, and typically, the reverse is also true (this shard is processed only by this record processor). However, your consumer should account for the possibility that a data record might be processed more than one time.This is because Kinesis Data Streams has "at least once" semantics, meaning that every data record from a shard is processed at least one time by a worker in your consumer. For more information about cases in which a particular shard may be processed by more than one worker, see Resharding, Scaling, and Parallel Processing.

```
1 initialize: function(initializeInput, completeCallback)
```

processRecords
The KCL calls this function with input that contains a list of data records from the shard specified to the `initialize` function. The record processor that you implement processes the data in these records according to

the semantics of your consumer. For example, the worker might perform a transformation on the data and then store the result in an S3 bucket.

```
1 processRecords : function (processRecordsInput, completeCallback)
```

In addition to the data itself, the record also contains a sequence number and partition key, which the worker can use when processing the data. For example, the worker could choose the S3 bucket in which to store the data based on the value of the partition key. The `record` dictionary exposes the following key-value pairs to access the record's data, sequence number, and partition key:

```
1 record.data
2 record.sequenceNumber
3 record.partitionKey
```

Note that the data is Base64-encoded.

In the basic sample, the function `processRecords` has code that shows how a worker can access the record's data, sequence number, and partition key.

Kinesis Data Streams requires the record processor to keep track of the records that have already been processed in a shard. The KCL takes care of this tracking for with a `checkpointer` object passed as `processRecordsInput.checkpointer`. Your record processor calls the `checkpointer.checkpoint` function to inform the KCL how far it has progressed in processing the records in the shard. In the event that the worker fails, the KCL uses this information when you restart the processing of the shard so that it continues from the last known processed record.

In the case of a split or merge operation, the KCL won't start processing the new shards until the processors for the original shards have called `checkpoint` to signal that all processing on the original shards is complete.

If you don't pass the sequence number to the `checkpoint` function, the KCL assumes that the call to `checkpoint` means that all records have been processed, up to the last record that was passed to the record processor. Therefore, the record processor should call `checkpoint` **only** after it has processed all the records in the list that was passed to it. Record processors do not need to call `checkpoint` on each call to `processRecords`. A processor could, for example, call `checkpoint` on every third call, or some event external to your record processor, such as a custom verification/validation service you've implemented.

You can optionally specify the exact sequence number of a record as a parameter to `checkpoint`. In this case, the KCL assumes that all records have been processed up to that record only.

The basic sample application shows the simplest possible call to the `checkpointer.checkpoint` function. You can add other checkpointing logic you need for your consumer at this point in the function.

shutdown

The KCL calls the `shutdown` function either when processing ends (`shutdownInput.reason` is `TERMINATE`) or the worker is no longer responding (`shutdownInput.reason` is `ZOMBIE`).

```
1 shutdown: function(shutdownInput, completeCallback)
```

Processing ends when the record processor does not receive any further records from the shard, because either the shard was split or merged, or the stream was deleted.

The KCL also passes a `shutdownInput.checkpointer` object to `shutdown`. If the shutdown reason is `TERMINATE`, you should make sure the record processor has finished processing any data records, and then call the `checkpoint` function on this interface.

Modify the Configuration Properties

The sample provides default values for the configuration properties. You can override any of these properties with your own values (see `sample.properties` in the basic sample).

Application Name

The KCL requires an application that this is unique among your applications, and among DynamoDB tables in the same region. It uses the application name configuration value in the following ways:

- All workers associated with this application name are assumed to be working together on the same stream. These workers may be distributed on multiple instances. If you run an additional instance of the same application code, but with a different application name, the KCL treats the second instance as an entirely separate application that is also operating on the same stream.
- The KCL creates a DynamoDB table with the application name and uses the table to maintain state information (such as checkpoints and worker-shard mapping) for the application. Each application has its own DynamoDB table. For more information, see Tracking Amazon Kinesis Data Streams Application State.

Set Up Credentials

You must make your AWS credentials available to one of the credential providers in the default credential providers chain. You can you use `AWSCredentialsProvider` property to set a credentials provider. The `sample.properties` file will need to make your credentials available to one of the credentials providers in the default credential providers chain. If you are running your consumer on an EC2 instance, we recommend that you configure the instance with an IAM role. AWS credentials that reflect the permissions associated with this IAM role are made available to applications on the instance through its instance metadata. This is the most secure way to manage credentials for a consumer application running on an EC2 instance.

The following example configures KCL to process a Kinesis data stream called "kclnodejssample" using the record processor supplied in `sample_kcl_app.js`:

```
1  # The Node.js executable
2  script
3  executableName = node sample_kcl_app.js
4  # The name of an Amazon Kinesis stream to process
5  streamName = kclnodejssample
6  # Unique KCL application name
7  applicationName = kclnodejssample
8  # Use default AWS credentials provider chain
9  AWSCredentialsProvider = DefaultAWSCredentialsProviderChain
10 # Read from the beginning of the stream
11 initialPositionInStream =  TRIM_HORIZON
```

Developing a Kinesis Client Library Consumer in .NET

You can use the Kinesis Client Library (KCL) to build applications that process data from your Kinesis data streams. The Kinesis Client Library is available in multiple languages. This topic discusses .NET.

The KCL is a Java library; support for languages other than Java is provided using a multi-language interface called the *MultiLangDaemon*. This daemon is Java-based and runs in the background when you are using a KCL language other than Java. Therefore, if you install the KCL for .NET and write your consumer app entirely in .NET, you still need Java installed on your system because of the MultiLangDaemon. Further, MultiLangDaemon has some default settings you may need to customize for your use case, for example the AWS region it connects to. For more information about the MultiLangDaemon, go to the KCL MultiLangDaemon project page on GitHub.

To download the .NET KCL from GitHub, go to Kinesis Client Library (.NET). To download sample code for a .NET KCL consumer application, go to the KCL for .NET sample consumer project page on GitHub.

You must complete the following tasks when implementing a KCL consumer application in .NET:

Topics

- Implement the IRecordProcessor Class Methods
- Modify the Configuration Properties

Implement the IRecordProcessor Class Methods

The consumer must implement the following methods for `IRecordProcessor`. The sample consumer provides implementations that you can use as a starting point (see the `SampleRecordProcessor` class in `SampleConsumer` `/AmazonKinesisSampleConsumer.cs`).

```
1 public void Initialize(InitializationInput input)
2 public void ProcessRecords(ProcessRecordsInput input)
3 public void Shutdown(ShutdownInput input)
```

Initialize
The KCL calls this method when the record processor is instantiated, passing a specific shard ID in the `input` parameter (`input.ShardId`). This record processor processes only this shard, and typically, the reverse is also true (this shard is processed only by this record processor). However, your consumer should account for the possibility that a data record might be processed more than one time. This is because Kinesis Data Streams has "at least once" semantics, meaning that every data record from a shard is processed at least one time by a worker in your consumer. For more information about cases in which a particular shard may be processed by more than one worker, see Resharding, Scaling, and Parallel Processing.

```
1 public void Initialize(InitializationInput input)
```

ProcessRecords
The KCL calls this method, passing a list of data records in the `input` parameter (`input.Records`) from the shard specified by the `Initialize` method. The record processor that you implement processes the data in these records according to the semantics of your consumer. For example, the worker might perform a transformation on the data and then store the result in an S3 bucket.

```
1 public void ProcessRecords(ProcessRecordsInput input)
```

In addition to the data itself, the record also contains a sequence number and partition key. The worker can use these values when processing the data. For example, the worker could choose the S3 bucket in which to store the data based on the value of the partition key. The `Record` class exposes the following to access the record's data, sequence number, and partition key:

```
1 byte[] Record.Data
2 string Record.SequenceNumber
3 string Record.PartitionKey
```

In the sample, the method `ProcessRecordsWithRetries` has code that shows how a worker can access the record's data, sequence number, and partition key.

Kinesis Data Streams requires the record processor to keep track of the records that have already been processed in a shard. The KCL takes care of this tracking for you by passing a `Checkpointer` object to `ProcessRecords` (`input.Checkpointer`). The record processor calls the `Checkpointer.Checkpoint` method to inform the KCL of how far it has progressed in processing the records in the shard. In the event that the worker fails, the KCL uses this information to restart the processing of the shard at the last known processed record.

In the case of a split or merge operation, the KCL won't start processing the new shards until the processors for the original shards have called `Checkpointer.Checkpoint` to signal that all processing on the original shards is complete.

If you don't pass a parameter, the KCL assumes that the call to `Checkpointer.Checkpoint` signifies that all records have been processed, up to the last record that was passed to the record processor. Therefore, the record processor should call `Checkpointer.Checkpoint` only after it has processed all the records in the list that was passed to it. Record processors do not need to call `Checkpointer.Checkpoint` on each call to `ProcessRecords`. A processor could, for example, call `Checkpointer.Checkpoint` on every third or fourth call. You can optionally specify the exact sequence number of a record as a parameter to `Checkpointer.Checkpoint`. In this case, the KCL assumes that records have been processed only up to that record.

In the sample, the private method `Checkpoint(Checkpointer checkpointer)` shows how to call the `Checkpointer.Checkpoint` method using appropriate exception handling and retry logic.

The KCL for .NET handles exceptions differently than other KCL language libraries in that it does not handle any exceptions that arise from processing the data records. Any uncaught exceptions from user code will crash the program.

Shutdown

The KCL calls the `Shutdown` method either when processing ends (the shutdown reason is `TERMINATE`) or the worker is no longer responding (the shutdown `input.Reason` value is `ZOMBIE`).

```
1 public void Shutdown(ShutdownInput input)
```

Processing ends when the record processor does not receive any further records from the shard, because the shard was split or merged, or the stream was deleted.

The KCL also passes a `Checkpointer` object to `shutdown`. If the shutdown reason is `TERMINATE`, the record processor should finish processing any data records, and then call the `checkpoint` method on this interface.

Modify the Configuration Properties

The sample consumer provides default values for the configuration properties. You can override any of these properties with your own values (see `SampleConsumer/kcl.properties`).

Application Name

The KCL requires an application that this is unique among your applications, and among DynamoDB tables in the same region. It uses the application name configuration value in the following ways:

- All workers associated with this application name are assumed to be working together on the same stream. These workers may be distributed on multiple instances. If you run an additional instance of the same application code, but with a different application name, the KCL treats the second instance as an entirely separate application that is also operating on the same stream.

- The KCL creates a DynamoDB table with the application name and uses the table to maintain state information (such as checkpoints and worker-shard mapping) for the application. Each application has its own DynamoDB table. For more information, see Tracking Amazon Kinesis Data Streams Application State.

Set Up Credentials

You must make your AWS credentials available to one of the credential providers in the default credential providers chain. You can you use `AWSCredentialsProvider` property to set a credentials provider. The sample.properties will need to make your credentials available to one of the credentials providers in the default credential providers chain. If you are running your consumer application on an EC2 instance, we recommend that you configure the instance with an IAM role. AWS credentials that reflect the permissions associated with this IAM role are made available to applications on the instance through its instance metadata. This is the most secure way to manage credentials for a consumer running on an EC2 instance.

The sample's properties file configures KCL to process a Kinesis data stream called "words" using the record processor supplied in `AmazonKinesisSampleConsumer.cs`.

Developing a Kinesis Client Library Consumer in Python

You can use the Kinesis Client Library (KCL) to build applications that process data from your Kinesis data streams. The Kinesis Client Library is available in multiple languages. This topic discusses Python.

The KCL is a Java library; support for languages other than Java is provided using a multi-language interface called the *MultiLangDaemon*. This daemon is Java-based and runs in the background when you are using a KCL language other than Java. Therefore, if you install the KCL for Python and write your consumer app entirely in Python, you still need Java installed on your system because of the MultiLangDaemon. Further, MultiLangDaemon has some default settings you may need to customize for your use case, for example the AWS region it connects to. For more information about the MultiLangDaemon, go to the KCL MultiLangDaemon project page on GitHub.

To download the Python KCL from GitHub, go to Kinesis Client Library (Python). To download sample code for a Python KCL consumer application, go to the KCL for Python sample project page on GitHub.

You must complete the following tasks when implementing a KCL consumer application in Python:

Topics

- Implement the RecordProcessor Class Methods
- Modify the Configuration Properties

Implement the RecordProcessor Class Methods

The `RecordProcess` class must extend the `RecordProcessorBase` to implement the following methods. The sample provides implementations that you can use as a starting point (see `sample_kclpy_app.py`).

```
1 def initialize(self, shard_id)
2 def process_records(self, records, checkpointer)
3 def shutdown(self, checkpointer, reason)
```

initialize
The KCL calls the `initialize` method when the record processor is instantiated, passing a specific shard ID as a parameter. This record processor processes only this shard, and typically, the reverse is also true (this shard is processed only by this record processor). However, your consumer should account for the possibility that a data record might be processed more than one time. This is because Kinesis Data Streams has "at least once" semantics, meaning that every data record from a shard is processed at least one time by a worker in your consumer. For more information about cases in which a particular shard may be processed by more than one worker, see Resharding, Scaling, and Parallel Processing.

```
1 def initialize(self, shard_id)
```

process_records
The KCL calls this method, passing a list of data record from the shard specified by the `initialize` method. The record processor you implement processes the data in these records according to the semantics of your consumer. For example, the worker might perform a transformation on the data and then store the result in an S3 bucket.

```
1 def process_records(self, records, checkpointer)
```

In addition to the data itself, the record also contains a sequence number and partition key. The worker can use these values when processing the data. For example, the worker could choose the S3 bucket in which to store the data based on the value of the partition key. The `record` dictionary exposes the following key-value pairs to access the record's data, sequence number, and partition key:

```
1  record.get('data')
2  record.get('sequenceNumber')
3  record.get('partitionKey')
```

Note that the data is Base64-encoded.

In the sample, the method `process_records` has code that shows how a worker can access the record's data, sequence number, and partition key.

Kinesis Data Streams requires the record processor to keep track of the records that have already been processed in a shard. The KCL takes care of this tracking for you by passing a `Checkpointer` object to `process_records`. The record processor calls the `checkpoint` method on this object to inform the KCL of how far it has progressed in processing the records in the shard. In the event that the worker fails, the KCL uses this information to restart the processing of the shard at the last known processed record.

In the case of a split or merge operation, the KCL won't start processing the new shards until the processors for the original shards have called `checkpoint` to signal that all processing on the original shards is complete.

If you don't pass a parameter, the KCL assumes that the call to `checkpoint` means that all records have been processed, up to the last record that was passed to the record processor. Therefore, the record processor should call `checkpoint` only after it has processed all the records in the list that was passed to it. Record processors do not need to call `checkpoint` on each call to `process_records`. A processor could, for example, call `checkpoint` on every third call. You can optionally specify the exact sequence number of a record as a parameter to `checkpoint`. In this case, the KCL assumes that all records have been processed up to that record only.

In the sample, the private method `checkpoint` shows how to call the `Checkpointer.checkpoint` method using appropriate exception handling and retry logic.

The KCL relies on `process_records` to handle any exceptions that arise from processing the data records. If an exception is thrown from `process_records`, the KCL skips over the data records that were passed to `process_records` prior to the exception; that is, these records are not re-sent to the record processor that threw the exception or to any other record processor in the consumer.

shutdown

The KCL calls the `shutdown` method either when processing ends (the shutdown reason is `TERMINATE`) or the worker is no longer responding (the shutdown `reason` is `ZOMBIE`).

```
1  def shutdown(self, checkpointer, reason)
```

Processing ends when the record processor does not receive any further records from the shard, because either the shard was split or merged, or the stream was deleted.

The KCL also passes a `Checkpointer` object to `shutdown`. If the shutdown `reason` is `TERMINATE`, the record processor should finish processing any data records, and then call the `checkpoint` method on this interface.

Modify the Configuration Properties

The sample provides default values for the configuration properties. You can override any of these properties with your own values (see `sample.properties`).

Application Name

The KCL requires an application that this is unique among your applications, and among DynamoDB tables in the same region. It uses the application name configuration value in the following ways:

- All workers associated with this application name are assumed to be working together on the same stream. These workers may be distributed on multiple instances. If you run an additional instance of the same application code, but with a different application name, the KCL treats the second instance as an entirely separate application that is also operating on the same stream.
- The KCL creates a DynamoDB table with the application name and uses the table to maintain state information (such as checkpoints and worker-shard mapping) for the application. Each application has its own DynamoDB table. For more information, see Tracking Amazon Kinesis Data Streams Application State.

Set Up Credentials

You must make your AWS credentials available to one of the credential providers in the default credential providers chain. You can you use `AWSCredentialsProvider` property to set a credentials provider. The sample.propertieswill need to make your credentials available to one of the credentials providers in the default credential providers chain. If you are running your consumer application on an EC2 instance, we recommend that you configure the instance with an IAM role. AWS credentials that reflect the permissions associated with this IAM role are made available to applications on the instance through its instance metadata. This is the most secure way to manage credentials for a consumer application running on an EC2 instance.

The sample's properties file configures KCL to process a Kinesis data stream called "words" using the record processor supplied in `sample_kclpy_app.py`.

Developing a Kinesis Client Library Consumer in Ruby

You can use the Kinesis Client Library (KCL) to build applications that process data from your Kinesis data streams. The Kinesis Client Library is available in multiple languages. This topic discusses Ruby.

The KCL is a Java library; support for languages other than Java is provided using a multi-language interface called the *MultiLangDaemon*. This daemon is Java-based and runs in the background when you are using a KCL language other than Java. Therefore, if you install the KCL for Ruby and write your consumer app entirely in Ruby, you still need Java installed on your system because of the MultiLangDaemon. Further, MultiLangDaemon has some default settings you may need to customize for your use case, for example the AWS region it connects to. For more information about the MultiLangDaemon, go to the KCL MultiLangDaemon project page on GitHub.

To download the Ruby KCL from GitHub, go to Kinesis Client Library (Ruby). To download sample code for a Ruby KCL consumer application, go to the KCL for Ruby sample project page on GitHub.

For more information about the KCL Ruby support library, see KCL Ruby Gems Documentation.

Developing Amazon Kinesis Data Streams Consumers Using the Amazon Kinesis Data Streams API with the AWS SDK for Java

You can develop consumers using the Amazon Kinesis Data Streams API with the AWS SDK for Java. If you are new to Kinesis Data Streams, start by becoming familiar with the concepts and terminology presented in What Is Amazon Kinesis Data Streams? and Getting Started Using Amazon Kinesis Data Streams.

These examples discuss the Kinesis Data Streams API and use the AWS SDK for Java to get data from a stream. However, for most use cases, you should prefer the Kinesis Data Streams KCL library. For more information, see Developing Amazon Kinesis Data Streams Consumers Using the Kinesis Client Library.

The Java example code in this chapter demonstrates how to perform basic Kinesis Data Streams API operations, and is divided up logically by operation type. These examples do not represent production-ready code, in that they do not check for all possible exceptions, or account for all possible security or performance considerations. Also, you can call the Kinesis Data Streams API using other different programming languages. For more information about all available AWS SDKs, see Start Developing with Amazon Web Services.

Each task has prerequisites; for example, you cannot add data to a stream until you have created a stream, which requires you to create a client. For more information, see Managing Kinesis Data Streams Using Java.

Getting Data from a Stream

The Kinesis Data Streams API provides the `getShardIterator` and `getRecords` methods to retrieve data from a stream. This is a pull model, where your code draws data directly from the shards of the stream.

We recommend that you use the record processor support provided by the Kinesis Client Library (KCL) to retrieve stream data in consumer applications. This is a push model, where you implement the code that processes the data. The KCL retrieves data records from the stream and delivers them to your application code. In addition, the KCL provides failover, recovery, and load balancing functionality. For more information, see Developing Amazon Kinesis Data Streams Consumers Using the Kinesis Client Library.

However, in some cases you might prefer to use the Kinesis Data Streams API with the AWS SDK for Java. For example, to implement custom tools for monitoring or debugging your streams.

Important
Changing the Data Retention Period

Using Shard Iterators

You retrieve records from the stream on a per-shard basis. For each shard, and for each batch of records that you retrieve from that shard, you need to obtain a *shard iterator*. The shard iterator is used in the `getRecordsRequest` object to specify the shard from which records are to be retrieved. The type associated with the shard iterator determines the point in the shard from which the records should be retrieved (see below for more details). Before you can work with the shard iterator, you'll need to retrieve the shard, discussed in Retrieving Shards from a Stream.

Obtain the initial shard iterator using the `getShardIterator` method. Obtain shard iterators for additional batches of records using the `getNextShardIterator` method of the `getRecordsResult` object returned by the `getRecords` method. A shard iterator is valid for five minutes. If you use a shard iterator while it is valid, you will get a new one. Note that each shard iterator remains valid for five minutes, even after it is used.

To obtain the initial shard iterator, instantiate `GetShardIteratorRequest` and pass it to the `getShardIterator` method. To configure the request, specify the stream and the shard ID. For information about how to obtain the streams in your AWS account, see Listing Streams. For information about how to obtain the shards in a stream, see Retrieving Shards from a Stream.

```
1 String shardIterator;
2 GetShardIteratorRequest getShardIteratorRequest = new GetShardIteratorRequest();
3 getShardIteratorRequest.setStreamName(myStreamName);
4 getShardIteratorRequest.setShardId(shard.getShardId());
5 getShardIteratorRequest.setShardIteratorType("TRIM_HORIZON");
6
7 GetShardIteratorResult getShardIteratorResult = client.getShardIterator(getShardIteratorRequest)
    ;
8 shardIterator = getShardIteratorResult.getShardIterator();
```

This sample code specifies `TRIM_HORIZON` as the iterator type when obtaining the initial shard iterator. This iterator type means that records should be returned beginning with the first record added to the shard — rather than beginning with the most recently added record, also known as the *tip*. The possible iterator types are the following:

- `AT_SEQUENCE_NUMBER`
- `AFTER_SEQUENCE_NUMBER`
- `AT_TIMESTAMP`
- `TRIM_HORIZON`
- `LATEST`

For more information, see ShardIteratorType.

Some iterator types require that you specify a sequence number in addition to the type. For example:

```
1 getShardIteratorRequest.setShardIteratorType("AT_SEQUENCE_NUMBER");
2 getShardIteratorRequest.setStartingSequenceNumber(specialSequenceNumber);
```

After you've obtained a record using **getRecords**, you can get the sequence number for the record by calling the record's **getSequenceNumber** method.

```
1 record.getSequenceNumber()
```

In addition, the code that adds records to the data stream can get the sequence number for an added record by calling getSequenceNumber on the result of **putRecord**.

```
1 lastSequenceNumber = putRecordResult.getSequenceNumber();
```

You can use sequence numbers to guarantee strictly increasing ordering of records. For more information, see the code sample in PutRecord Example.

Using GetRecords

After you've obtained the shard iterator, instantiate a **GetRecordsRequest** object. Specify the iterator for the request using the **setShardIterator** method.

Optionally, you can also set the number of records to retrieve using the **setLimit** method. The number of records returned by **getRecords** is always equal to or less than this limit. If you do not specify this limit, **getRecords** returns 10 MB of retrieved records. The sample code below sets this limit to 25 records.

If no records are returned, that means no data records are currently available from this shard at the sequence number referenced by the shard iterator. When this situation occurs, your application should wait for an amount of time that's appropriate for the data sources for the stream, but at least one second. Then try to get data from the shard again using the shard iterator returned by the preceding call to **getRecords**. Note that there is about a three-second latency from the time that a record is added to the stream to the time that it is available from **getRecords**.

Pass the **getRecordsRequest** to the **getRecords** method and capture the returned value as a **getRecordsResult** object. To get the data records, call the **getRecords** method on the **getRecordsResult** object.

```
1 GetRecordsRequest getRecordsRequest = new GetRecordsRequest();
2 getRecordsRequest.setShardIterator(shardIterator);
3 getRecordsRequest.setLimit(25);
4
5 GetRecordsResult getRecordsResult = client.getRecords(getRecordsRequest);
6 List<Record> records = getRecordsResult.getRecords();
```

To prepare for another call to getRecords, obtain the next shard iterator from getRecordsResult.

```
1 shardIterator = getRecordsResult.getNextShardIterator();
```

For best results, sleep for at least one second (1000 milliseconds) between calls to getRecords to avoid exceeding the limit on getRecords frequency.

```
1 try {
2   Thread.sleep(1000);
3 }
4 catch (InterruptedException e) {}
```

Typically, you should call getRecords in a loop, even when you're retrieving a single record in a test scenario. A single call to getRecords might return an empty record list, even when the shard contains more records at later sequence numbers. When this occurs, the NextShardIterator returned along with the empty record list references a later sequence number in the shard, and successive getRecords calls will eventually return the records. The following sample demonstrates the use of a loop.

Example: getRecords
The following code sample reflects the getRecords tips in this section, including making calls in a loop.

```
1 // Continuously read data records from a shard
2 List<Record> records;
3
4 while (true) {
5
6   // Create a new getRecordsRequest with an existing shardIterator
7   // Set the maximum records to return to 25
8   GetRecordsRequest getRecordsRequest = new GetRecordsRequest();
9   getRecordsRequest.setShardIterator(shardIterator);
10  getRecordsRequest.setLimit(25);
11
12  GetRecordsResult result = client.getRecords(getRecordsRequest);
13
14  // Put the result into record list. The result can be empty.
15  records = result.getRecords();
16
17  try {
18    Thread.sleep(1000);
19  }
20  catch (InterruptedException exception) {
21    throw new RuntimeException(exception);
22  }
23
24  shardIterator = result.getNextShardIterator();
25 }
```

If you are using the Kinesis Client Library, note that the KCL might make multiple calls before returning data. This behavior is by design and does not indicate a problem with the KCL or your data.

Adapting to a Reshard

If `getRecordsResult.getNextShardIterator` returns `null`, it indicates the following: a shard split or merge has occurred that involved this shard, this shard is now in a `CLOSED` state, and you have read all available data records from this shard.

In this scenario, you should re-enumerate the shards in the stream to pick up the new shards that were created by the split or merge.

In the case of a split, the two new shards both have `parentShardId` equal to the shard ID of the shard that you were processing previously. The value of `adjacentParentShardId` for both of these shards is `null`.

In the case of a merge, the single new shard created by the merge has `parentShardId` equal to shard ID of one of the parent shards and `adjacentParentShardId` equal to the shard ID of the other parent shard. Your application has already read all the data from one of these shards; this is the shard for which `getRecordsResult`.`getNextShardIterator` returned `null`. If the order of the data is important to your application, you should ensure that it reads all the data from the other parent shard as well, before reading any new data from the child shard created by the merge.

If you are using multiple processors to retrieve data from the stream, say one processor per shard, and a shard split or merge occurs, you should adjust the number of processors up or down to adapt to the change in the number of shards.

For more information about resharding, including a discussion of shards states—such as `CLOSED`—see Resharding a Stream.

Troubleshooting Amazon Kinesis Data Streams Consumers

Topics

- Some Kinesis Data Streams Records are Skipped When Using the Kinesis Client Library
- Records Belonging to the Same Shard are Processed by Different Record Processors at the Same Time
- Consumer Application is Reading at a Slower Rate Than Expected
- GetRecords Returns Empty Records Array Even When There is Data in the Stream
- Shard Iterator Expires Unexpectedly
- Consumer Record Processing Falling Behind
- Unauthorized KMS master key permission error

Some Kinesis Data Streams Records are Skipped When Using the Kinesis Client Library

The most common cause of skipped records is an unhandled exception thrown from `processRecords`. The Kinesis Client Library (KCL) relies on your `processRecords` code to handle any exceptions that arise from processing the data records. Any exception thrown from `processRecords` is absorbed by the KCL. To avoid infinite retries on a recurring failure, the KCL does not resend the batch of records processed at the time of the exception. The KCL then calls `processRecords` for the next batch of data records without restarting the record processor. This effectively results in consumer applications observing skipped records. To prevent skipped records, handle all exceptions within `processRecords` appropriately.

Records Belonging to the Same Shard are Processed by Different Record Processors at the Same Time

For any running Kinesis Client Library (KCL) application, a shard only has one owner. However, multiple record processors may temporarily process the same shard. In the case of a worker instance that loses network connectivity, the KCL assumes that the unreachable worker is no longer processing records, after the failover time expires, and directs other worker instances to take over. For a brief period, new record processors and record processors from the unreachable worker may process data from the same shard.

You should set a failover time that is appropriate for your application. For low-latency applications, the 10-second default may represent the maximum time you want to wait. However, in cases where you expect connectivity issues such as making calls across geographical areas where connectivity could be lost more frequently, this number may be too low.

Your application should anticipate and handle this scenario, especially because network connectivity is usually restored to the previously unreachable worker. If a record processor has its shards taken by another record processor, it must handle the following two cases to perform graceful shutdown:

1. After the current call to `processRecords` is completed, the KCL invokes the shutdown method on the record processor with shutdown reason 'ZOMBIE'. Your record processors are expected to clean up any resources as appropriate and then exit.

2. When you attempt to checkpoint from a 'zombie' worker, the KCL throws `ShutdownException`. After receiving this exception, your code is expected to exit the current method cleanly.

For more information, see Handling Duplicate Records.

Consumer Application is Reading at a Slower Rate Than Expected

The most common reasons for read throughput being slower than expected are as follows:

1. Multiple consumer applications have total reads exceeding the per-shard limits. For more information, see Amazon Kinesis Data Streams Limits. In this case, increase the number of shards in the Kinesis data stream.

2. The limit that specifies the maximum number of GetRecords per call may have been configured with a low value. If you are using the KCL, you may have configured the worker with a low value for the `maxRecords` property. In general, we recommend using the system defaults for this property.

3. The logic inside your `processRecords` call may be taking longer than expected for a number of possible reasons; the logic may be CPU intensive, I/O blocking, or bottlenecked on synchronization. To test if this is true, test run empty record processors and compare the read throughput. For information about how to keep up with the incoming data, see Resharding, Scaling, and Parallel Processing.

If you have only one consumer application, it is always possible to read at least two times faster than the put rate. That's because you can write up to 1,000 records per second for writes, up to a maximum total data write rate of 1 MB per second (including partition keys). Each open shard can support up to 5 transactions per second for reads, up to a maximum total data read rate of 2 MB per second. Note that each read (GetRecords call) gets a batch of records. The size of the data returned by GetRecords varies depending on the utilization of the shard. The maximum size of data that GetRecords can return is 10 MB. If a call returns that limit, subsequent calls made within the next 5 seconds throw `ProvisionedThroughputExceededException`.

GetRecords Returns Empty Records Array Even When There is Data in the Stream

Consuming, or getting records is a pull model. Developers are expected to call GetRecords in a continuous loop with no back-offs. Every call to GetRecords also returns a `ShardIterator` value, which must be used in the next iteration of the loop.

The GetRecords operation does not block. Instead, it returns immediately; with either relevant data records or with an empty `Records` element. An empty `Records` element is returned under two conditions:

1. There is no more data currently in the shard.

2. There is no data near the part of the shard pointed to by the `ShardIterator`.

The latter condition is subtle, but is a necessary design tradeoff to avoid unbounded seek time (latency) when retrieving records. Thus, the stream-consuming application should loop and call GetRecords, handling empty records as a matter of course.

In a production scenario, the only time the continuous loop should be exited is when the `NextShardIterator` value is `NULL`. When `NextShardIterator` is `NULL`, it means that the current shard has been closed and the `ShardIterator`value would otherwise point past the last record. If the consuming application never calls Split-Shard or MergeShards, the shard remains open and the calls to GetRecords never return a `NextShardIterator` value that is `NULL`.

If you use the Kinesis Client Library (KCL), the above consumption pattern is abstracted for you. This includes automatic handling of a set of shards that dynamically change. With the KCL, the developer only supplies the logic to process incoming records. This is possible because the library makes continuous calls to GetRecords for you.

Shard Iterator Expires Unexpectedly

A new shard iterator is returned by every GetRecords request (as `NextShardIterator`), which you then use in the next GetRecords request (as `ShardIterator`). Typically, this shard iterator does not expire before you use it. However, you may find that shard iterators expire because you have not called GetRecords for more than 5 minutes, or because you've performed a restart of your consumer application.

If the shard iterator expires immediately, before you can use it, this might indicate that the DynamoDB table used by Kinesis does not have enough capacity to store the lease data. This situation is more likely to happen if you have a large number of shards. To solve this problem, increase the write capacity assigned to the shard table. For more information, see Tracking Amazon Kinesis Data Streams Application State.

Consumer Record Processing Falling Behind

For most use cases, consumer applications are reading the latest data from the stream. In certain circumstances, consumer reads may fall behind, which may not be desired. After you identify how far behind your consumers are reading, look at the most common reasons why consumers fall behind.

Start with the `GetRecords.IteratorAgeMilliseconds` metric, which tracks the read position across all shards and consumers in the stream. Note that if an iterator's age passes 50% of the retention period (by default 24 hours, configurable up to 7 days), there is risk for data loss due to record expiration. A quick stopgap solution is to increase the retention period. This stops the loss of important data while you troubleshoot the issue further. For more information, see Monitoring the Amazon Kinesis Data Streams Service with Amazon CloudWatch. Next, identify how far behind your consumer application is reading from each shard using a custom CloudWatch metric emitted by the Kinesis Client Library (KCL), `MillisBehindLatest`. For more information, see Monitoring the Kinesis Client Library with Amazon CloudWatch.

Here are the most common reasons consumers can fall behind:

- Sudden large increases to `GetRecords.IteratorAgeMilliseconds` or `MillisBehindLatest` usually indicate a transient problem, such as API operation failures to a downstream application. You should investigate these sudden increases if either of the metrics consistently display this behavior.
- A gradual increase to these metrics indicates that a consumer is not keeping up with the stream because it is not processing records fast enough. The most common root causes for this behavior are insufficient physical resources or record processing logic that has not scaled with an increase in stream throughput. You can verify this behavior by looking at the other custom CloudWatch metrics that the KCL emits associated with the `processTask` operation, including `RecordProcessor.processRecords.Time`, `Success`, and `RecordsProcessed`.
  - If you see an increase in the `processRecords.Time` metric that correlates with increased throughput, you should analyze your record processing logic to identify why it is not scaling with the increased throughput.
  - If you see an increase to the `processRecords.Time` values that are not correlated with increased throughput, check to see if you are making any blocking calls in the critical path, which are often the cause of slowdowns in record processing. An alternative approach is to increase your parallelism by increasing the number of shards. Finally, confirm you have an adequate amount of physical resources (memory, CPU utilization, etc.) on the underlying processing nodes during peak demand.

Unauthorized KMS master key permission error

This error occurs when a consumer application reads from an encrypted stream without permissions on the KMS master key. To assign permissions to an application to access a KMS key, see Using Key Policies in AWS KMS and Using IAM Policies with AWS KMS.

Advanced Topics for Amazon Kinesis Data Streams Consumers

Learn how to optimize your Amazon Kinesis Data Streams consumer.

Topics

- Tracking Amazon Kinesis Data Streams Application State
- Low-Latency Processing
- Using AWS Lambda with the Kinesis Producer Library
- Resharding, Scaling, and Parallel Processing
- Handling Duplicate Records
- Recovering from Failures in Amazon Kinesis Data Streams
- Handling Startup, Shutdown, and Throttling

Tracking Amazon Kinesis Data Streams Application State

For each Amazon Kinesis Data Streams application, the KCL uses a unique Amazon DynamoDB table to keep track of the application's state. Because the KCL uses the name of the Amazon Kinesis Data Streams application to create the name of the table, each application name must be unique.

You can view the table using the Amazon DynamoDB console while the application is running.

If the Amazon DynamoDB table for your Amazon Kinesis Data Streams application does not exist when the application starts up, one of the workers creates the table and calls the `describeStream` method to populate the table. For more information, see Application State Data.

Important
Your account is charged for the costs associated with the DynamoDB table, in addition to the costs associated with Kinesis Data Streams itself.

Throughput

If your Amazon Kinesis Data Streams application receives provisioned-throughput exceptions, you should increase the provisioned throughput for the DynamoDB table. The KCL creates the table with a provisioned throughput of 10 reads per second and 10 writes per second, but this might not be sufficient for your application. For example, if your Amazon Kinesis Data Streams application does frequent checkpointing or operates on a stream that is composed of many shards, you might need more throughput.

For information about provisioned throughput in DynamoDB, see Provisioned Throughput in Amazon DynamoDB and Working with Tables in the *Amazon DynamoDB Developer Guide*.

Application State Data

Each row in the DynamoDB table represents a shard that is being processed by your application. The hash key for the table is the shard ID.

In addition to the shard ID, each row also includes the following data:

- **checkpoint:** The most recent checkpoint sequence number for the shard. This value is unique across all shards in the stream.
- **checkpointSubSequenceNumber:** When using the Kinesis Producer Library's aggregation feature, this is an extension to **checkpoint** that tracks individual user records within the Kinesis record.
- **leaseCounter:** Used for lease versioning so that workers can detect that their lease has been taken by another worker.
- **leaseKey:** A unique identifier for a lease. Each lease is particular to a shard in the stream and is held by one worker at a time.
- **leaseOwner:** The worker that is holding this lease.
- **ownerSwitchesSinceCheckpoint:** How many times this lease has changed workers since the last time a checkpoint was written.
- **parentShardId:** Used to ensure that the parent shard is fully processed before processing starts on the child shards. This ensures that records are processed in the same order they were put into the stream.

Low-Latency Processing

Propagation delay is defined as the end-to-end latency from the moment a record is written to the stream until it is read by a consumer application. This delay varies depending upon a number of factors, but it is primarily affected by the polling interval of consumer applications.

For most applications, we recommend polling each shard one time per second per application. This enables you to have multiple consumer applications processing a stream concurrently without hitting Amazon Kinesis Data Streams limits of 5 `GetRecords` calls per second. Additionally, processing larger batches of data tends to be more efficient at reducing network and other downstream latencies in your application.

The KCL defaults are set to follow the best practice of polling every 1 second. This default results in average propagation delays that are typically below 1 second.

Kinesis Data Streams records are available to be read immediately after they are written. There are some use cases that need to take advantage of this and require consuming data from the stream as soon as it is available. You can significantly reduce the propagation delay by overriding the KCL default settings to poll more frequently, as shown in the following examples.

Java KCL configuration code:

```
1 kinesisClientLibConfiguration = new
2        KinesisClientLibConfiguration(applicationName,
3        streamName,
4        credentialsProvider,
5        workerId).withInitialPositionInStream(initialPositionInStream).
               withIdleTimeBetweenReadsInMillis(250);
```

Property file setting for Python and Ruby KCL:

```
1 idleTimeBetweenReadsInMillis = 250
```

Note
Because Kinesis Data Streams has a limit of 5 `GetRecords` calls per second, per shard, setting the `idleTimeBetweenReadsInMillis` property lower than 200ms may result in your application observing the `ProvisionedThroughputExceededException` exception. Too many of these exceptions can result in exponential back-offs and thereby cause significant unexpected latencies in processing. If you set this property to be at or just above 200 ms and have more than one processing application, you will experience similar throttling.

Using AWS Lambda with the Kinesis Producer Library

The Kinesis Producer Library (KPL) aggregates small user-formatted records into larger records up to 1 MB to make better use of Amazon Kinesis Data Streams throughput. While the KCL for Java supports deaggregating these records, you need to use a special module to deaggregate records when using AWS Lambda as the consumer of your streams. You can obtain the necessary project code and instructions from GitHub at Kinesis Producer Library Deaggregation Modules for AWS Lambda. The components in this project give you the ability to process KPL serialized data within AWS Lambda, in Java, Node.js and Python. These components can also be used as part of a multi-lang KCL application.

Resharding, Scaling, and Parallel Processing

Resharding enables you to increase or decrease the number of shards in a stream in order to adapt to changes in the rate of data flowing through the stream. Resharding is typically performed by an administrative application that monitors shard data-handling metrics. Although the KCL itself doesn't initiate resharding operations, it is designed to adapt to changes in the number of shards that result from resharding.

As noted in Tracking Amazon Kinesis Data Streams Application State, the KCL tracks the shards in the stream using an Amazon DynamoDB table. When new shards are created as a result of resharding, the KCL discovers the new shards and populates new rows in the table. The workers automatically discover the new shards and create processors to handle the data from them. The KCL also distributes the shards in the stream across all the available workers and record processors.

The KCL ensures that any data that existed in shards prior to the resharding is processed first. After that data has been processed, data from the new shards is sent to record processors. In this way, the KCL preserves the order in which data records were added to the stream for a particular partition key.

Example: Resharding, Scaling, and Parallel Processing

The following example illustrates how the KCL helps you handle scaling and resharding:

- For example, if your application is running on one EC2 instance, and is processing one Kinesis data stream that has four shards. This one instance has one KCL worker and four record processors (one record processor for every shard). These four record processors run in parallel within the same process.
- Next, if you scale the application to use another instance, you have two instances processing one stream that has four shards. When the KCL worker starts up on the second instance, it load-balances with the first instance, so that each instance now processes two shards.
- If you then decide to split the four shards into five shards. The KCL again coordinates the processing across instances: one instance processes three shards, and the other processes two shards. A similar coordination occurs when you merge shards.

Typically, when you use the KCL, you should ensure that the number of instances does not exceed the number of shards (except for failure standby purposes). Each shard is processed by exactly one KCL worker and has exactly one corresponding record processor, so you never need multiple instances to process one shard. However, one worker can process any number of shards, so it's fine if the number of shards exceeds the number of instances.

To scale up processing in your application, you should test a combination of these approaches:

- Increasing the instance size (because all record processors run in parallel within a process)
- Increasing the number of instances up to the maximum number of open shards (because shards can be processed independently)
- Increasing the number of shards (which increases the level of parallelism)

Note that you can use Auto Scaling to automatically scale your instances based on appropriate metrics. For more information, see the Amazon EC2 Auto Scaling User Guide.

When resharding increases the number of shards in the stream, the corresponding increase in the number of record processors increases the load on the EC2 instances that are hosting them. If the instances are part of an Auto Scaling group, and the load increases sufficiently, the Auto Scaling group adds more instances to handle the increased load. You should configure your instances to launch your Amazon Kinesis Data Streams application at startup, so that additional workers and record processors become active on the new instance right away.

For more information about resharding, see Resharding a Stream.

Handling Duplicate Records

There are two primary reasons why records may be delivered more than one time to your Amazon Kinesis Data Streams application: producer retries and consumer retries. Your application must anticipate and appropriately handle processing individual records multiple times.

Producer Retries

Consider a producer that experiences a network-related timeout after it makes a call to `PutRecord`, but before it can receive an acknowledgement from Amazon Kinesis Data Streams. The producer cannot be sure if the record was delivered to Kinesis Data Streams. Assuming that every record is important to the application, the producer would have been written to retry the call with the same data. If both `PutRecord` calls on that same data were successfully committed to Kinesis Data Streams, then there will be two Kinesis Data Streams records. Although the two records have identical data, they also have unique sequence numbers. Applications that need strict guarantees should embed a primary key within the record to remove duplicates later when processing. Note that the number of duplicates due to producer retries is usually low compared to the number of duplicates due to consumer retries.

Note
If you use the AWS SDK `PutRecord`, the default configuration retries a failed `PutRecord` call up to three times.

Consumer Retries

Consumer (data processing application) retries happen when record processors restart. Record processors for the same shard restart in the following cases:

1. A worker terminates unexpectedly

2. Worker instances are added or removed

3. Shards are merged or split

4. The application is deployed

In all these cases, the shards-to-worker-to-record-processor mapping is continuously updated to load balance processing. Shard processors that were migrated to other instances restart processing records from the last checkpoint. This results in duplicated record processing as shown in the example below. For more information about load-balancing, see Resharding, Scaling, and Parallel Processing.

Example: Consumer Retries Resulting in Redelivered Records

In this example, you have an application that continuously reads records from a stream, aggregates records into a local file, and uploads the file to Amazon S3. For simplicity, assume there is only 1 shard and 1 worker processing the shard. Consider the following example sequence of events, assuming that the last checkpoint was at record number 10000:

1. A worker reads the next batch of records from the shard, records 10001 to 20000.

2. The worker then passes the batch of records to the associated record processor.

3. The record processor aggregates the data, creates an Amazon S3 file, and uploads the file to Amazon S3 successfully.

4. Worker terminates unexpectedly before a new checkpoint can occur.

5. Application, worker, and record processor restart.

6. Worker now begins reading from the last successful checkpoint, in this case 10001.

Thus, records 10001-20000 are consumed more than one time.

Being Resilient to Consumer Retries

Even though records may be processed more than one time, your application may want to present the side effects as if records were processed only one time (idempotent processing). Solutions to this problem vary in complexity and accuracy. If the destination of the final data can handle duplicates well, we recommend relying on the final destination to achieve idempotent processing. For example, with Elasticsearch you can use a combination of versioning and unique IDs to prevent duplicated processing.

In the example application in the previous section, it continuously reads records from a stream, aggregates records into a local file, and uploads the file to Amazon S3. As illustrated, records 10001 -20000 are consumed more than one time resulting in multiple Amazon S3 files with the same data. One way to mitigate duplicates from this example is to ensure that step 3 uses the following scheme:

1. Record Processor uses a fixed number of records per Amazon S3 file, such as 5000.

2. The file name uses this schema: Amazon S3 prefix, shard-id, and `First-Sequence-Num`. In this case, it could be something like `sample-shard000001-10001`.

3. After you upload the Amazon S3 file, checkpoint by specifying `Last-Sequence-Num`. In this case, you would checkpoint at record number 15000.

With this scheme, even if records are processed more than one time, the resulting Amazon S3 file has the same name and has the same data. The retries only result in writing the same data to the same file more than one time.

In the case of a reshard operation, the number of records left in the shard may be less than your desired fixed number needed. In this case, your `shutdown()` method has to flush the file to Amazon S3 and checkpoint on the last sequence number. The above scheme is compatible with reshard operations as well.

Recovering from Failures in Amazon Kinesis Data Streams

Failure can occur at the following levels when you use an Amazon Kinesis Data Streams application to process data from a stream:

- A record processor could fail
- A worker could fail, or the instance of the application that instantiated the worker could fail
- An EC2 instance that is hosting one or more instances of the application could fail

Record Processor Failure

The worker invokes record processor methods using Java ExecutorService tasks. If a task fails, the worker retains control of the shard that the record processor was processing. The worker starts a new record processor task to process that shard. For more information, see Read Throttling.

Worker or Application Failure

If a worker — or an instance of the Amazon Kinesis Data Streams application — fails, you should detect and handle the situation. For example, if the `Worker.run` method throws an exception, you should catch and handle it.

If the application itself fails, you should detect this and restart it. When the application starts up, it instantiates a new worker, which in turn instantiates new record processors that are automatically assigned shards to process. These could be the same shards that these record processors were processing before the failure, or shards that are new to these processors.

If the worker or application fails but you do not detect the failure, and there are other instances of the application running on other EC2 instances, the workers on these instances handle the failure: they create additional record processors to process the shards that are no longer being processed by the failed worker. The load on these other EC2 instances increases accordingly.

The scenario described here assumes that although the worker or application has failed, the hosting EC2 instance is still running and is therefore not restarted by an Auto Scaling group.

Amazon EC2 Instance Failure

We recommend that you run the EC2 instances for your application in an Auto Scaling group. This way, if one of the EC2 instances fails, the Auto Scaling group automatically launches a new instance to replace it. You should configure the instances to launch your Amazon Kinesis Data Streams application at startup.

Handling Startup, Shutdown, and Throttling

Here are some additional considerations to incorporate into the design of your Amazon Kinesis Data Streams application.

Topics

- Starting Up Data Producers and Data Consumers
- Shutting Down an Amazon Kinesis Data Streams Application
- Read Throttling

Starting Up Data Producers and Data Consumers

By default, the KCL begins reading records from the tip of the stream;, which is the most recently added record. In this configuration, if a data-producing application adds records to the stream before any receiving record processors are running, the records are not read by the record processors after they start up.

To change the behavior of the record processors so that it always reads data from the beginning of the stream, set the following value in the properties file for your Amazon Kinesis Data Streams application:

```
1 initialPositionInStream = TRIM_HORIZON
```

Amazon Kinesis Data Streams keeps records for 24 to 168 hours. This time frame is called the *retention period*. Setting the starting position to the `TRIM_HORIZON` will start the record processor with the oldest data in the stream, as defined by the retention period. Even with the `TRIM_HORIZON` setting, if a record processor were to start after a greater time has passed than the retention period, then some of the records in the stream will no longer be available. For this reason, you should always have consumer applications reading from the stream and use the CloudWatch metric `GetRecords.IteratorAgeMilliseconds` to monitor that applications are keeping up with incoming data.

In some scenarios, it may be fine for record processors to miss the first few records in the stream. For example, you might run some initial records through the stream to test that the stream is working end-to-end as expected. After doing this initial verification, you would then start your workers and begin to put production data into the stream.

For more information about the `TRIM_HORIZON` setting, see Using Shard Iterators.

Shutting Down an Amazon Kinesis Data Streams Application

When your Amazon Kinesis Data Streams application has completed its intended task, you should shut it down by terminating the EC2 instances on which it is running. You can terminate the instances using the AWS Management Console or the AWS CLI.

After shutting down your Amazon Kinesis Data Streams application, you should delete the Amazon DynamoDB table that the KCL used to track the application's state.

Read Throttling

The throughput of a stream is provisioned at the shard level. Each shard has a read throughput of up to 5 transactions per second for reads, up to a maximum total data read rate of 2 MB per second. If an application (or a group of applications operating on the same stream) attempts to get data from a shard at a faster rate, Kinesis Data Streams throttles the corresponding Get operations.

In an Amazon Kinesis Data Streams application, if a record processor is processing data faster than the limit — such as in the case of a failover — throttling occurs. Because the Kinesis Client Library manages the interactions between the application and Kinesis Data Streams, throttling exceptions occur in the KCL code rather than in the application code. However, because the KCL logs these exceptions, you see them in the logs.

If you find that your application is throttled consistently, you should consider increasing the number of shards for the stream.

Managing Kinesis Data Streams Using Java

These examples discuss the Amazon Kinesis Data Streams API and use the AWS SDK for Java to create, delete, and work with a Kinesis data stream.

The Java example code in this chapter demonstrates how to perform basic Kinesis Data Streams API operations, and are divided up logically by operation type. These examples do not represent production-ready code, in that they do not check for all possible exceptions, or account for all possible security or performance considerations. Also, you can call the Kinesis Data Streams API using other different programming languages. For more information about all available AWS SDKs, see Start Developing with Amazon Web Services.

Topics

- Creating a Stream
- Listing Streams
- Retrieving Shards from a Stream
- Deleting a Stream
- Resharding a Stream
- Changing the Data Retention Period

Creating a Stream

Use the following steps to create your Kinesis data stream.

Build the Kinesis Data Streams Client

Before you can work with Kinesis data streams you must build a client object. The following Java code instantiates a client builder and uses it to set the Region, credentials, and the client configuration. It then builds a client object.

```
1 AmazonKinesisClientBuilder clientBuilder = AmazonKinesisClientBuilder.standard();
2
3 clientBuilder.setRegion(regionName);
4 clientBuilder.setCredentials(credentialsProvider);
5 clientBuilder.setClientConfiguration(config);
6
7 AmazonKinesis client = clientBuilder.build();
```

For more information, see Kinesis Data Streams Regions and Endpoints in the *AWS General Reference*.

Create the Stream

Now that you have created your Kinesis Data Streams client, you can create a stream to work with, which you can accomplish with the Kinesis Data Streams console, or programmatically. To create a stream programmatically, instantiate a `CreateStreamRequest` object and specify a name for the stream and the number of shards for the stream to use.

```
1 CreateStreamRequest createStreamRequest = new CreateStreamRequest();
2 createStreamRequest.setStreamName( myStreamName );
3 createStreamRequest.setShardCount( myStreamSize );
```

The stream name identifies the stream. The name is scoped to the AWS account used by the application. It is also scoped by Region. That is, two streams in two different AWS accounts can have the same name, and two streams in the same AWS account but in two different Regions can have the same name, but not two streams on the same account and in the same Region.

The throughput of the stream is a function of the number of shards; more shards are required for greater provisioned throughput. More shards also increase the cost that AWS charges for the stream. For more information, about calculating an appropriate number of shards for your application, see Determining the Initial Size of a Kinesis Data Stream.

After the `createStreamRequest` object is configured, create a stream by calling the `createStream` method on the client. After calling `createStream`, wait for the stream to reach the `ACTIVE` state before performing any operations on the stream. To check the state of the stream, call the `describeStream` method. However, `describeStream` throws an exception if the stream does not exist. Therefore, enclose the `describeStream` call in a `try/catch` block.

```
1 client.createStream( createStreamRequest );
2 DescribeStreamRequest describeStreamRequest = new DescribeStreamRequest();
3 describeStreamRequest.setStreamName( myStreamName );
4
5 long startTime = System.currentTimeMillis();
6 long endTime = startTime + ( 10 * 60 * 1000 );
7 while ( System.currentTimeMillis() < endTime ) {
8   try {
```

```
 9      Thread.sleep(20 * 1000);
10    }
11    catch ( Exception e ) {}
12
13    try {
14      DescribeStreamResult describeStreamResponse = client.describeStream( describeStreamRequest )
           ;
15      String streamStatus = describeStreamResponse.getStreamDescription().getStreamStatus();
16      if ( streamStatus.equals( "ACTIVE" ) ) {
17        break;
18      }
19      //
20      // sleep for one second
21      //
22      try {
23        Thread.sleep( 1000 );
24      }
25      catch ( Exception e ) {}
26    }
27    catch ( ResourceNotFoundException e ) {}
28  }
29  if ( System.currentTimeMillis() >= endTime ) {
30    throw new RuntimeException( "Stream " + myStreamName + " never went active" );
31  }
```

Listing Streams

As described in the previous section, streams are scoped to the AWS account associated with the AWS credentials used to instantiate the Kinesis Data Streams client and also to the Region specified for the client. An AWS account could have many streams active at one time. You can list your streams in the Kinesis Data Streams console, or programmatically. The code in this section shows how to list all the streams for your AWS account.

```
1 ListStreamsRequest listStreamsRequest = new ListStreamsRequest();
2 listStreamsRequest.setLimit(20);
3 ListStreamsResult listStreamsResult = client.listStreams(listStreamsRequest);
4 List<String> streamNames = listStreamsResult.getStreamNames();
```

This code example first creates a new instance of `ListStreamsRequest` and calls its `setLimit` method to specify that a maximum of 20 streams should be returned for each call to `listStreams`. If you do not specify a value for `setLimit`, Kinesis Data Streams returns a number of streams less than or equal to the number in the account. The code then passes `listStreamsRequest` to the `listStreams` method of the client. The return value `listStreams` is stored in a `ListStreamsResult` object. The code calls the `getStreamNames` method on this object and stores the returned stream names in the `streamNames` list. Note that Kinesis Data Streams might return fewer streams than specified by the specified limit even if there are more streams than that in the account and Region. To ensure that you retrieve all the streams, use the `getHasMoreStreams` method as described in the next code example.

```
1 while (listStreamsResult.getHasMoreStreams())
2 {
3     if (streamNames.size() > 0) {
4         listStreamsRequest.setExclusiveStartStreamName(streamNames.get(streamNames.size() - 1));
5     }
6     listStreamsResult = client.listStreams(listStreamsRequest);
7     streamNames.addAll(listStreamsResult.getStreamNames());
8 }
```

This code calls the `getHasMoreStreams` method on `listStreamsRequest` to check if there are additional streams available beyond the ones returned in the initial call to `listStreams`. If so, the code calls the `setExclusiveStartStreamName` method with the name of the last stream that was returned in the previous call to `listStreams`. The `setExclusiveStartStreamName` method causes the next call to `listStreams` to start after that stream. The group of stream names returned by that call is then added to the `streamNames` list. This process continues until all the stream names have been collected in the list.

The streams returned by `listStreams` can be in one of the following states:

- CREATING
- ACTIVE
- UPDATING
- DELETING

You can check the state of a stream using the `describeStream` method, as shown in the previous section, Creating a Stream.

Retrieving Shards from a Stream

The response object returned by the `describeStream` method enables you to retrieve information about the shards that comprise the stream. To retrieve the shards, call the `getShards` method on this object. This method might not return all the shards from the stream in a single call. In the following code, we check the `getHasMoreShards` method on `getStreamDescription` to see if there are additional shards that were not returned. If so, that is, if this method returns `true`, we continue to call `getShards` in a loop, adding each new batch of returned shards to our list of shards. The loop exits when `getHasMoreShards` returns `false`; that is, all shards have been returned. Note that `getShards` does not return shards that are in the `EXPIRED` state. For more information about shard states, including the `EXPIRED` state, see Data Routing, Data Persistence, and Shard State after a Reshard.

```
1  DescribeStreamRequest describeStreamRequest = new DescribeStreamRequest();
2  describeStreamRequest.setStreamName( myStreamName );
3  List<Shard> shards = new ArrayList<>();
4  String exclusiveStartShardId = null;
5  do {
6      describeStreamRequest.setExclusiveStartShardId( exclusiveStartShardId );
7      DescribeStreamResult describeStreamResult = client.describeStream( describeStreamRequest );
8      shards.addAll( describeStreamResult.getStreamDescription().getShards() );
9      if (describeStreamResult.getStreamDescription().getHasMoreShards() && shards.size() > 0) {
10         exclusiveStartShardId = shards.get(shards.size() - 1).getShardId();
11     } else {
12         exclusiveStartShardId = null;
13     }
14 } while ( exclusiveStartShardId != null );
```

Deleting a Stream

You can delete a stream with the Kinesis Data Streams console, or programmatically. To delete a stream programmatically, use `DeleteStreamRequest` as shown in the following code.

```
1 DeleteStreamRequest deleteStreamRequest = new DeleteStreamRequest();
2 deleteStreamRequest.setStreamName(myStreamName);
3 client.deleteStream(deleteStreamRequest);
```

You should shut down any applications that are operating on the stream before you delete it. If an application attempts to operate on a deleted stream, it receives `ResourceNotFound` exceptions. Also, if you subsequently create a new stream that has the same name as your previous stream, and applications that were operating on the previous stream are still running, these applications might try to interact with the new stream as though it was the previous stream—which would result in unpredictable behavior.

Resharding a Stream

Important

You can reshard your stream using the UpdateShardCount API. Otherwise, you can continue to perform splits and merges as explained here.

Kinesis Data Streams supports *resharding*, which enables you to adjust the number of shards in your stream in order to adapt to changes in the rate of data flow through the stream. Resharding is considered an advanced operation. If you are new to Kinesis Data Streams, return to this subject after you are familiar with all the other aspects of Kinesis Data Streams.

There are two types of resharding operations: shard split and shard merge. In a shard split, you divide a single shard into two shards. In a shard merge, you combine two shards into a single shard. Resharding is always "pairwise" in the sense that you cannot split into more than two shards in a single operation, and you cannot merge more than two shards in a single operation. The shard or pair of shards that the resharding operation acts on are referred to as *parent* shards. The shard or pair of shards that result from the resharding operation are referred to as *child* shards.

Splitting increases the number of shards in your stream and therefore increases the data capacity of the stream. Because you are charged on a per-shard basis, splitting increases the cost of your stream. Similarly, merging reduces the number of shards in your stream and therefore decreases the data capacity—and cost—of the stream.

Resharding is typically performed by an administrative application which is distinct from the producer (put) applications, and the consumer (get) applications. Such an administrative application monitors the overall performance of the stream based on metrics provided by CloudWatch or based on metrics collected from the producers and consumers. The administrative application would also need a broader set of IAM permissions than the consumers or producers because the consumers and producers usually should not need access to the APIs used for resharding. For more information about IAM permissions for Kinesis Data Streams, see Controlling Access to Amazon Kinesis Data Streams Resources Using IAM.

Topics

- Strategies for Resharding
- Splitting a Shard
- Merging Two Shards
- After Resharding

Strategies for Resharding

The purpose of resharding is to enable your stream to adapt to changes in the rate of data flow. You split shards to increase the capacity (and cost) of your stream. You merge shards to reduce the cost (and capacity) of your stream.

One approach to resharding could be to simply split every shard in the stream—which would double the stream's capacity. However, this might provide more additional capacity than you actually need and therefore create unnecessary cost.

You can also use metrics to determine which are your "hot" or "cold" shards, that is, shards that are receiving much more data, or much less data, than expected. You could then selectively split the hot shards to increase capacity for the hash keys that target those shards. Similarly, you could merge cold shards to make better use of their unused capacity.

You can obtain some performance data for your stream from the CloudWatch metrics that Kinesis Data Streams publishes. However, you can also collect some of your own metrics for your streams. One approach would be to log the hash key values generated by the partition keys for your data records. Recall that you specify the partition key at the time that you add the record to the stream.

```
1 putRecordRequest.setPartitionKey( String.format( "myPartitionKey" ) );
```

Kinesis Data Streams uses MD5 to compute the hash key from the partition key. Because you specify the partition key for the record, you could use MD5 to compute the hash key value for that record and log it.

You could also log the IDs of the shards that your data records are assigned to. The shard ID is available by using the `getShardId` method of the `putRecordResults` object returned by the `putRecords` method, and the `putRecordResult` object returned by the `putRecord` method.

```
1 String shardId = putRecordResult.getShardId();
```

With the shard IDs and the hash key values, you can determine which shards and hash keys are receiving the most or least traffic. You can then use resharding to provide more or less capacity, as appropriate for these keys.

Splitting a Shard

To split a shard, you need to specify how hash key values from the parent shard should be redistributed to the child shards. When you add a data record to a stream, it is assigned to a shard based on a hash key value. The hash key value is the MD5 hash of the partition key that you specify for the data record at the time that you add the data record to the stream; data records that have the same partition key also have the same hash key value.

The possible hash key values for a given shard constitute a set of ordered contiguous non-negative integers. This range of possible hash key values is given by:

```
1 shard.getHashKeyRange().getStartingHashKey();
2 shard.getHashKeyRange().getEndingHashKey();
```

When you split the shard, you specify a value in this range. That hash key value and all higher hash key values are distributed to one of the child shards. All the lower hash key values are distributed to the other child shard.

The following code demonstrates a shard split operation that redistributes the hash keys evenly between each of the child shards, essentially splitting the parent shard in half. This is just one possible way of dividing the parent shard. You could, for example, split the shard so that the lower one-third of the keys from the parent go to one child shard and the upper two-thirds of the keys go to other child shard. However, for many applications, splitting shards in half is an effective approach.

The code assumes that `myStreamName` holds the name of your stream and the object variable `shard` holds the shard to split. Begin by instantiating a new `splitShardRequest` object and setting the stream name and shard ID.

```
1 SplitShardRequest splitShardRequest = new SplitShardRequest();
2 splitShardRequest.setStreamName(myStreamName);
3 splitShardRequest.setShardToSplit(shard.getShardId());
```

Determine the hash key value that is half-way between the lowest and highest values in the shard. This is the starting hash key value for the child shard that will contain the upper half of the hash keys from the parent shard. Specify this value in the `setNewStartingHashKey` method. You need specify only this value; Kinesis Data Streams automatically distributes the hash keys below this value to the other child shard that is created by the split. The last step is to call the `splitShard` method on the Kinesis Data Streams client.

```
1 BigInteger startingHashKey = new BigInteger(shard.getHashKeyRange().getStartingHashKey());
2 BigInteger endingHashKey   = new BigInteger(shard.getHashKeyRange().getEndingHashKey());
3 String newStartingHashKey  = startingHashKey.add(endingHashKey).divide(new BigInteger("2")).
    toString();
4
5 splitShardRequest.setNewStartingHashKey(newStartingHashKey);
6 client.splitShard(splitShardRequest);
```

The first step after this procedure is shown in Waiting for a Stream to Become Active Again.

Merging Two Shards

A shard merge operation takes two specified shards and combines them into a single shard. After the merge, the single child shard receives data for all hash key values covered by the two parent shards.

Shard Adjacency

In order to merge two shards, the shards must be *adjacent*. Two shards are considered adjacent if the union of the hash key ranges for the two shards form a contiguous set with no gaps. For example, if you have two shards, one with a hash key range of 276...381 and the other with a hash key range of 382...454, then you could merge these two shards into a single shard that would have a hash key range of 276...454.

To take another example, if you have two shards, one with a hash key range of 276..381 and the other with a hash key range of 455...560, then you could not merge these two shards because there would be one or more shards between these two that cover the range 382..454.

The set of all OPEN shards in a stream—as a group—always spans the entire range of MD5 hash key values. For more information about shard states—such as CLOSED—see Data Routing, Data Persistence, and Shard State after a Reshard.

To identify shards that are candidates for merging, you should filter out all shards that are in a CLOSED state. Shards that are OPEN—that is, not CLOSED—have an ending sequence number of null. You can test the ending sequence number for a shard using:

```
1 if( null == shard.getSequenceNumberRange().getEndingSequenceNumber() )
2 {
3   // Shard is OPEN, so it is a possible candidate to be merged.
4 }
```

After filtering out the closed shards, sort the remaining shards by the highest hash key value supported by each shard. You can retrieve this value using:

```
1 shard.getHashKeyRange().getEndingHashKey();
```

If two shards are adjacent in this filtered, sorted list, they can be merged.

Code for the Merge Operation

The following code merges two shards. The code assumes that myStreamName holds the name of your stream and the object variables shard1 and shard2 hold the two adjacent shards to merge.

For the merge operation, begin by instantiating a new mergeShardsRequest object. Specify the stream name with the setStreamName method. Then specify the two shards to merge using the setShardToMerge and setAdjacentShardToMerge methods. Finally, call the mergeShards method on Kinesis Data Streams client to carry out the operation.

```
1 MergeShardsRequest mergeShardsRequest = new MergeShardsRequest();
2 mergeShardsRequest.setStreamName(myStreamName);
3 mergeShardsRequest.setShardToMerge(shard1.getShardId());
4 mergeShardsRequest.setAdjacentShardToMerge(shard2.getShardId());
5 client.mergeShards(mergeShardsRequest);
```

The first step after this procedure is shown in Waiting for a Stream to Become Active Again.

After Resharding

After any kind of resharding procedure, and before normal record processing resumes, other procedures and considerations are required. The following sections describe these.

Topics

- Waiting for a Stream to Become Active Again
- Data Routing, Data Persistence, and Shard State after a Reshard

Waiting for a Stream to Become Active Again

After you call a resharding operation, either `splitShard` or `mergeShards`, you need to wait for the stream to become active again. The code to use is the same as when you wait for a stream to become active after creating a stream. That code is reproduced below.

```
1  DescribeStreamRequest describeStreamRequest = new DescribeStreamRequest();
2  describeStreamRequest.setStreamName( myStreamName );
3
4  long startTime = System.currentTimeMillis();
5  long endTime = startTime + ( 10 * 60 * 1000 );
6  while ( System.currentTimeMillis() < endTime )
7  {
8    try {
9      Thread.sleep(20 * 1000);
10   }
11   catch ( Exception e ) {}
12
13   try {
14     DescribeStreamResult describeStreamResponse = client.describeStream( describeStreamRequest )
          ;
15     String streamStatus = describeStreamResponse.getStreamDescription().getStreamStatus();
16     if ( streamStatus.equals( "ACTIVE" ) ) {
17       break;
18     }
19     //
20     // sleep for one second
21     //
22     try {
23       Thread.sleep( 1000 );
24     }
25     catch ( Exception e ) {}
26   }
27   catch ( ResourceNotFoundException e ) {}
28 }
29 if ( System.currentTimeMillis() >= endTime )
30 {
31   throw new RuntimeException( "Stream " + myStreamName + " never went active" );
32 }
```

Data Routing, Data Persistence, and Shard State after a Reshard

Kinesis Data Streams is a real-time data streaming service, which is to say that your applications should assume that data is flowing continuously through the shards in your stream. When you reshard, data records that

134

were flowing to the parent shards are re-routed to flow to the child shards based on the hash key values that the data-record partition keys map to. However, any data records that were in the parent shards before the reshard remain in those shards. In other words, the parent shards do not disappear when the reshard occurs; they persist along with the data they contained prior to the reshard. The data records in the parent shards are accessible using the `getShardIterator` and `getRecords` operations in the Kinesis Data Streams API, or through the Kinesis Client Library.

Note

Data records are accessible from the time they are added to the stream to the current retention period. This holds true regardless of any changes to the shards in the stream during that time period. For more information about a stream's retention period, see Changing the Data Retention Period.

In the process of resharding, a parent shard transitions from an `OPEN` state to a `CLOSED` state to an `EXPIRED` state.

- **OPEN**: Before a reshard operation, a parent shard is in the `OPEN` state, which means that data records can be both added to the shard and retrieved from the shard.
- **CLOSED**: After a reshard operation, the parent shard transitions to a `CLOSED` state. This means that data records are no longer added to the shard. Data records that would have been added to this shard are now added to a child shard instead. However, data records can still be retrieved from the shard for a limited time.
- **EXPIRED**: After the stream's retention period has expired, all the data records in the parent shard have expired and are no longer accessible. At this point, the shard itself transitions to an `EXPIRED` state. Calls to `getStreamDescription().getShards` to enumerate the shards in the stream do not include `EXPIRED` shards in the list shards returned. For more information about a stream's retention period, see Changing the Data Retention Period.

After the reshard has occurred and the stream is again in an `ACTIVE` state, you could immediately begin to read data from the child shards. However, the parent shards that remain after the reshard could still contain data that you haven't read yet that was added to the stream prior to the reshard. If you read data from the child shards before having read all data from the parent shards, you could read data for a particular hash key out of the order given by the data records' sequence numbers. Therefore, assuming that the order of the data is important, you should, after a reshard, always continue to read data from the parent shards until it is exhausted, and only then begin reading data from the child shards. When `getRecordsResult.getNextShardIterator` returns `null`, it indicates that you have read all the data in the parent shard. If you are reading data using the Kinesis Client Library, the library ensures that you receive the data in order even if a reshard occurs.

Changing the Data Retention Period

Kinesis Data Streams supports changes to the data record retention period of your stream. A Kinesis data stream is an ordered sequence of data records meant to be written to and read from in real-time. Data records are therefore stored in shards in your stream temporarily. The time period from when a record is added to when it is no longer accessible is called the *retention period*. A Kinesis data stream stores records from 24 hours by default, up to 168 hours.

You can increase the retention period up to 168 hours using the IncreaseStreamRetentionPeriod operation, and decrease the retention period down to a minimum of 24 hours using the DecreaseStreamRetentionPeriod operation. The request syntax for both operations includes the stream name and the retention period in hours. Finally, you can check the current retention period of a stream by calling the DescribeStream operation.

Both operations are easy to operate. An example of changing the retention period is shown using the AWS CLI.

```
1 aws kinesis increase-stream-retention-period --stream-name retentionPeriodDemo --retention-
    period-hours 72
```

Kinesis Data Streams stops making records inaccessible at the old retention period within several minutes of increasing the retention period. For example, changing the retention period from 24 hours to 48 hours means records added to the stream 23 hours 55 minutes prior will still be available after 24 hours have passed.

Kinesis Data Streams almost immediately makes records older than the new retention period inaccessible upon decreasing the retention period. Therefore, great care should be taken when calling the DecreaseStreamRetentionPeriod operation.

You should set your data retention period to ensure that your consumers are able to read data before it expires, if problems occur. You should carefully consider all possibilities such as an issue with your record processing logic or a downstream dependency being down for a long period of time. The retention period should be thought of as a safety net to allow more time for your data consumers to recover. The retention period API operations allow you to set this up proactively or to respond to operational events reactively.

Additional charges apply for streams with a retention period set above 24 hours. For more information, see Amazon Kinesis Data Streams Pricing.

Managing Kinesis Streams Using the Console

The following procedures show you how to create, delete, and work with an Kinesis stream using the AWS Management Console.

To create a stream

1. Open the Kinesis console at https://console.aws.amazon.com/kinesis.

2. Choose **Go to Streams**.

3. Choose **Create Stream**.

4. Type a name for the stream (for example, StockTradeStream).

5. Specify the number of shards. If you need help, expand **Estimate the number of shards you'll need**.

6. Choose **Create stream**.

To list your streams

1. Open the Kinesis console at https://console.aws.amazon.com/kinesis.

2. Choose **Go to Streams**.

3. (Optional) To view more details for a stream, choose the name of the stream.

To edit a stream

1. Open the Kinesis console at https://console.aws.amazon.com/kinesis.

2. Choose **Go to Streams**.

3. Choose the name of the stream.

4. To scale the shard capacity, do the following:

    1. Under **Shards**, choose **Edit**.

    2. Specify the new number of shards.

    3. Choose **Save**.

5. To edit the data retention period, do the following:

    1. Under **Data retention period**, choose **Edit**.

    2. Specify a period between 24-168 hours. Records are stored in the stream for this period of time. Note that additional charges apply for periods greater than 24 hours. For more information, see Amazon Kinesis Data Streams pricing.

    3. Choose **Save**.

6. To enable or disable shard-level metrics, do the following:

    1. Under **Shard level metrics**, choose **Edit**.

    2. Select the metrics to monitor. For more information, see Enhanced Shard-level Metrics.

    3. Choose **Save**.

To delete your streams

1. Open the Kinesis console at https://console.aws.amazon.com/kinesis.

2. Choose **Go to Streams**.

3. Select the checkbox next to the streams to delete.

4. Choose **Actions, Delete**.

5. When prompted for confirmation, choose **Delete**.

Monitoring Amazon Kinesis Data Streams

You can monitor Amazon Kinesis Data Streams using the following features:

- CloudWatch metrics— Kinesis Data Streams sends Amazon CloudWatch custom metrics with detailed monitoring for each stream.
- Kinesis Agent— The Kinesis Agent publishes custom CloudWatch metrics to help assess if the agent is working as expected.
- API logging— Kinesis Data Streams uses AWS CloudTrail to log API calls and store the data in an Amazon S3 bucket.
- Kinesis Client Library— Kinesis Data Streams Client Library (KCL) provides metrics per shard, worker, and KCL application.
- Kinesis Producer Library— Kinesis Data Streams Producer Library (KPL) provides metrics per shard, worker, and KPL application.

Monitoring the Amazon Kinesis Data Streams Service with Amazon CloudWatch

Amazon Kinesis Data Streams and Amazon CloudWatch are integrated so that you can collect, view, and analyze CloudWatch metrics for your Kinesis data streams. For example, to keep track of shard usage, you can monitor the `PutRecords.Bytes` and `GetRecords.Bytes` metrics and compare them to the number of shards in the stream.

The metrics that you configure for your streams are automatically collected and pushed to CloudWatch every minute. Metrics are archived for two weeks; after that period, the data is discarded.

The following table describes basic stream-level and enhanced shard-level monitoring for Kinesis streams.

Type	Description
Basic (stream-level)	Stream-level data is sent automatically every minute at no charge.
Enhanced (shard-level)	Shard-level data is sent every minute for an additional cost. To get this level of data, you must specifically enable it for the stream using the EnableEnhancedMonitoring operation. For information about pricing, see the Amazon CloudWatch product page.

Amazon Kinesis Data Streams Dimensions and Metrics

Kinesis Data Streams sends metrics to CloudWatch at two levels; the stream level and, optionally, the shard level. Stream-level metrics are for most common monitoring use cases in normal conditions. Shard-level metrics are for specific monitoring tasks, usually related to troubleshooting, and are enabled using the EnableEnhancedMonitoring operation.

For an explanation of the statistics gathered from CloudWatch metrics, see CloudWatch Statistics in the *Amazon CloudWatch User Guide.*

Topics

- Basic Stream-level Metrics
- Enhanced Shard-level Metrics
- Dimensions for Amazon Kinesis Data Streams Metrics
- Recommended Amazon Kinesis Data Streams Metrics

Basic Stream-level Metrics

The `AWS/Kinesis` namespace includes the following stream-level metrics.

Kinesis Data Streams sends these stream-level metrics to CloudWatch every minute. These metrics are always available.

Metric	Description
GetRecords.Bytes	The number of bytes retrieved from the Kinesis stream, measured over the specified time period. Minimum, Maximum, and Average statistics represent the bytes in a single `GetRecords` operation for the stream in the specified time period. Shard-level metric name: `OutgoingBytes` Dimensions: StreamName Statistics: Minimum, Maximum, Average, Sum, Samples Units: Bytes
GetRecords.IteratorAge	This metric is deprecated. Use `GetRecords.IteratorAgeMilliseconds`.
GetRecords.IteratorAgeMilliseconds	The age of the last record in all `GetRecords` calls made against an Kinesis stream, measured over the specified time period. Age is the difference between the current time and when the last record of the `GetRecords` call was written to the stream. The Minimum and Maximum statistics can be used to track the progress of Kinesis consumer applications. A value of zero indicates that the records being read are completely caught up with the stream. Shard-level metric name: `IteratorAgeMilliseconds` Dimensions: StreamName Statistics: Minimum, Maximum, Average, Samples Units: Milliseconds
GetRecords.Latency	The time taken per `GetRecords` operation, measured over the specified time period. Dimensions: StreamName Statistics: Minimum, Maximum, Average Units: Milliseconds
GetRecords.Records	The number of records retrieved from the shard, measured over the specified time period. Minimum, Maximum, and Average statistics represent the records in a single `GetRecords` operation for the stream in the specified time period. Shard-level metric name: `OutgoingRecords` Dimensions: StreamName Statistics: Minimum, Maximum, Average, Sum, Samples Units: Count
GetRecords.Success	The number of successful `GetRecords` operations per stream, measured over the specified time period. Dimensions: StreamName Statistics: Average, Sum, Samples Units: Count

Metric	Description
IncomingBytes	The number of bytes successfully put to the Kinesis stream over the specified time period. This metric includes bytes from `PutRecord` and `PutRecords` operations. Minimum, Maximum, and Average statistics represent the bytes in a single put operation for the stream in the specified time period. Shard-level metric name: `IncomingBytes` Dimensions: StreamName Statistics: Minimum, Maximum, Average, Sum, Samples Units: Bytes
IncomingRecords	The number of records successfully put to the Kinesis stream over the specified time period. This metric includes record counts from `PutRecord` and `PutRecords` operations. Minimum, Maximum, and Average statistics represent the records in a single put operation for the stream in the specified time period. Shard-level metric name: `IncomingRecords` Dimensions: StreamName Statistics: Minimum, Maximum, Average, Sum, Samples Units: Count
PutRecord.Bytes	The number of bytes put to the Kinesis stream using the `PutRecord` operation over the specified time period. Dimensions: StreamName Statistics: Minimum, Maximum, Average, Sum, Samples Units: Bytes
PutRecord.Latency	The time taken per `PutRecord` operation, measured over the specified time period. Dimensions: StreamName Statistics: Minimum, Maximum, Average Units: Milliseconds
PutRecord.Success	The number of successful `PutRecord` operations per Kinesis stream, measured over the specified time period. Average reflects the percentage of successful writes to a stream. Dimensions: StreamName Statistics: Average, Sum, Samples Units: Count
PutRecords.Bytes	The number of bytes put to the Kinesis stream using the `PutRecords` operation over the specified time period. Dimensions: StreamName Statistics: Minimum, Maximum, Average, Sum, Samples Units: Bytes
PutRecords.Latency	The time taken per `PutRecords` operation, measured over the specified time period. Dimensions: StreamName Statistics: Minimum, Maximum, Average Units: Milliseconds
PutRecords.Records	The number of successful records in a `PutRecords` operation per Kinesis stream, measured over the specified time period. Dimensions: StreamName Statistics: Minimum, Maximum, Average, Sum, Samples Units: Count

Metric	Description
PutRecords.Success	The number of `PutRecords` operations where at least one record succeeded, per Kinesis stream, measured over the specified time period. Dimensions: StreamName Statistics: Average, Sum, Samples Units: Count
ReadProvisionedThroughputExceeded	The number of `GetRecords` calls throttled for the stream over the specified time period. The most commonly used statistic for this metric is Average. When the Minimum statistic has a value of 1, all records were throttled for the stream during the specified time period. When the Maximum statistic has a value of 0 (zero), no records were throttled for the stream during the specified time period. Shard-level metric name: `ReadProvisionedThroughputExceeded` Dimensions: StreamName Statistics: Minimum, Maximum, Average, Sum, Samples Units: Count
WriteProvisionedThroughputExceeded	The number of records rejected due to throttling for the stream over the specified time period. This metric includes throttling from `PutRecord` and `PutRecords` operations. The most commonly used statistic for this metric is Average. When the Minimum statistic has a non-zero value, records were being throttled for the stream during the specified time period. When the Maximum statistic has a value of 0 (zero), no records were being throttled for the stream during the specified time period. Shard-level metric name: `WriteProvisionedThroughputExceeded` Dimensions: StreamName Statistics: Minimum, Maximum, Average, Sum, Samples Units: Count

Enhanced Shard-level Metrics

The `AWS/Kinesis` namespace includes the following shard-level metrics.

Kinesis sends the following shard-level metrics to CloudWatch every minute. These metrics are not enabled by default. There is a charge for enhanced metrics emitted from Kinesis. For more information, see Amazon CloudWatch Pricing under the heading *Amazon CloudWatch Custom Metrics*. The charges are given per shard per metric per month.

Metric	Description
IncomingBytes	The number of bytes successfully put to the shard over the specified time period. This metric includes bytes from `PutRecord` and `PutRecords` operations. Minimum, Maximum, and Average statistics represent the bytes in a single put operation for the shard in the specified time period. Stream-level metric name: `IncomingBytes` Dimensions: StreamName, ShardId Statistics: Minimum, Maximum, Average, Sum, Samples Units: Bytes
IncomingRecords	The number of records successfully put to the shard over the specified time period. This metric includes record counts from `PutRecord` and `PutRecords` operations. Minimum, Maximum, and Average statistics represent the records in a single put operation for the shard in the specified time period. Stream-level metric name: `IncomingRecords` Dimensions: StreamName, ShardId Statistics: Minimum, Maximum, Average, Sum, Samples Units: Count
IteratorAgeMilliseconds	The age of the last record in all `GetRecords` calls made against a shard, measured over the specified time period. Age is the difference between the current time and when the last record of the `GetRecords` call was written to the stream. The Minimum and Maximum statistics can be used to track the progress of Kinesis consumer applications. A value of 0 (zero) indicates that the records being read are completely caught up with the stream. Stream-level metric name: `GetRecords.IteratorAgeMilliseconds` Dimensions: StreamName, ShardId Statistics: Minimum, Maximum, Average, Samples Units: Milliseconds
OutgoingBytes	The number of bytes retrieved from the shard, measured over the specified time period. Minimum, Maximum, and Average statistics represent the bytes in a single `GetRecords` operation for the shard in the specified time period. Stream-level metric name: `GetRecords.Bytes` Dimensions: StreamName, ShardId Statistics: Minimum, Maximum, Average, Sum, Samples Units: Bytes

Metric	Description
OutgoingRecords	The number of records retrieved from the shard, measured over the specified time period. Minimum, Maximum, and Average statistics represent the records in a single `GetRecords` operation for the shard in the specified time period. Stream-level metric name: `GetRecords.Records` Dimensions: StreamName, ShardId Statistics: Minimum, Maximum, Average, Sum, Samples Units: Count
ReadProvisionedThroughputExceeded	The number of `GetRecords` calls throttled for the shard over the specified time period. This exception count covers all dimensions of the following limits: 5 reads per shard per second or 2 MB per second per shard. The most commonly used statistic for this metric is Average. When the Minimum statistic has a value of 1, all records were throttled for the shard during the specified time period. When the Maximum statistic has a value of 0 (zero), no records were throttled for the shard during the specified time period. Stream-level metric name: `ReadProvisionedThroughputExceeded` Dimensions: StreamName, ShardId Statistics: Minimum, Maximum, Average, Sum, Samples Units: Count
WriteProvisionedThroughputExceeded	The number of records rejected due to throttling for the shard over the specified time period. This metric includes throttling from `PutRecord` and `PutRecords` operations and covers all dimensions of the following limits: 1,000 records per second per shard or 1 MB per second per shard. The most commonly used statistic for this metric is Average. When the Minimum statistic has a non-zero value, records were being throttled for the shard during the specified time period. When the Maximum statistic has a value of 0 (zero), no records were being throttled for the shard during the specified time period. Stream-level metric name: `WriteProvisionedThroughputExceeded` Dimensions: StreamName, ShardId Statistics: Minimum, Maximum, Average, Sum, Samples Units: Count

Dimensions for Amazon Kinesis Data Streams Metrics

You can use the following dimensions to filter the metrics for Amazon Kinesis Data Streams.

Dimension	Description
StreamName	The name of the Kinesis stream.
ShardId	The shard ID within the Kinesis stream.

Recommended Amazon Kinesis Data Streams Metrics

There are several Amazon Kinesis Data Streams metrics of particular interest to the majority of Kinesis Data Streams customers. The following list provides recommended metrics and their uses.

Metric	Usage Notes
GetRecords.IteratorAgeMilliseconds	Tracks the read position across all shards and consumers in the stream. Note that if an iterator's age passes 50% of the retention period (by default 24 hours, configurable up to 7 days), there is risk for data loss due to record expiration. We advise the use of CloudWatch alarms on the Maximum statistic to alert you before this loss is a risk. For an example scenario that uses this metric, see Consumer Record Processing Falling Behind.
ReadProvisionedThroughputExceeded	When your consumer side record processing is falling behind, it is sometimes difficult to know where the bottleneck is. Use this metric to determine if your reads are being throttled due to exceeding your read throughput limits. The most commonly used statistic for this metric is Average.
WriteProvisionedThroughputExceeded	This is for the same purpose as the ReadProvisionedThroughputExceeded metric, but for the producer (put) side of the stream. The most commonly used statistic for this metric is Average.
PutRecord.Success, PutRecords.Success	We advise the use of CloudWatch alarms on the Average statistic to indicate if records are failing to the stream. Choose one or both put types depending on what your producer uses. If using the Kinesis Producer Library (KPL), use PutRecords.Success.
GetRecords.Success	We advise the use of CloudWatch alarms on the Average statistic to indicate if records are failing from the stream.

Accessing Amazon CloudWatch Metrics for Kinesis Data Streams

You can monitor metrics for Kinesis Data Streams using the CloudWatch console, the command line, or the CloudWatch API. The following procedures show you how to access metrics using these different methods.

To access metrics using the CloudWatch console

1. Open the CloudWatch console at https://console.aws.amazon.com/cloudwatch/.

2. From the navigation bar, select a region.

146

3. In the navigation pane, choose **Metrics**.

4. In the **CloudWatch Metrics by Category** pane, choose **Kinesis Metrics**.

5. Click the relevant row to view the statistics for the specified **MetricName** and **StreamName**.

   Note: Most console statistic names match the corresponding CloudWatch metric names listed above, with the exception of **Read Throughput** and **Write Throughput**. These statistics are calculated over 5-minute intervals: **Write Throughput** monitors the `IncomingBytes` CloudWatch metric, and **Read Throughput** monitors `GetRecords.Bytes`.

6. (Optional) In the graph pane, select a statistic and a time period and then create a CloudWatch alarm using these settings.

To access metrics using the AWS CLI

Use the list-metrics and get-metric-statistics commands.

To access metrics using the CloudWatch CLI

Use the mon-list-metrics and mon-get-stats commands.

To access metrics using the CloudWatch API

Use the ListMetrics and GetMetricStatistics operations.

Monitoring Kinesis Data Streams Agent Health with Amazon Cloud-Watch

The agent publishes custom CloudWatch metrics with a namespace of **AWSKinesisAgent** to help assess if the agent is submitting data into Kinesis Data Streams as specified, and is healthy and consuming the appropriate amount of CPU and memory resources on the data producer. Metrics such as number of records and bytes sent are useful to understand the rate at which the agent is submitting data to the stream. When these metrics fall below expected thresholds by some percentage or drop to zero, it could indicate configuration issues, network errors, or agent health issues. Metrics such as on-host CPU and memory consumption and agent error counters indicate data producer resource usage, and provide insights into potential configuration or host errors. Finally, the agent also logs service exceptions to help investigate agent issues. These metrics are reported in the region specified in the agent configuration setting `cloudwatch.endpoint`. For more information about agent configuration, see Agent Configuration Settings.

Monitoring with CloudWatch

The Kinesis Data Streams agent sends the following metrics to CloudWatch.

Metric	Description
BytesSent	The number of bytes sent to Kinesis Data Streams over the specified time period. Units: Bytes
RecordSendAttempts	The number of records attempted (either first time, or as a retry) in a call to `PutRecords` over the specified time period. Units: Count
RecordSendErrors	The number of records that returned failure status in a call to `PutRecords`, including retries, over the specified time period. Units: Count
ServiceErrors	The number of calls to `PutRecords` that resulted in a service error (other than a throttling error) over the specified time period. Units: Count

Logging Amazon Kinesis Data Streams API Calls Using AWS Cloud-Trail

Amazon Kinesis Data Streams is integrated with AWS CloudTrail, which captures API calls made by or on behalf of Kinesis Data Streams and delivers the log files to the Amazon S3 bucket that you specify. The API calls can be made indirectly by using the Kinesis Data Streams console or directly by using the Kinesis Data Streams API. Using the information collected by CloudTrail, you can determine what request was made to Kinesis Data Streams, the source IP address from which the request was made, who made the request, when it was made, and so on. To learn more about CloudTrail, including how to configure and enable it, see the *AWS CloudTrail User Guide*.

Kinesis Data Streams and CloudTrail

CloudTrail logging is enabled by default. Calls made to Kinesis Data Streams actions are tracked in log files. Records for Kinesis Data Streams are written in a log file, together with records from any other AWS service enabled for CloudTrail logging. CloudTrail determines when to create and write to a new file based on the specified time period and file size.

The following actions are supported:

- AddTagsToStream
- CreateStream
- DecreaseStreamRetentionPeriod
- DeleteStream
- DescribeLimits
- DescribeStream
- DescribeStreamSummary
- DisableEnhancedMonitoring
- EnableEnhancedMonitoring
- IncreaseStreamRetentionPeriod
- ListStreams
- ListTagsForStream
- MergeShards
- RemoveTagsFromStream
- SplitShard
- StartStreamEncryption
- StopStreamEncryption
- UpdateShardCount

Each log entry contains information about who generated the request. For example, if a request is made to create a stream (CreateStream), the user identity of the person or service that made the request is logged. The user identity information helps you determine whether the request was made with root or IAM user credentials, with temporary security credentials for a role or federated user, or by another AWS service. For more information, see the userIdentity Element in the *AWS CloudTrail User Guide*.

You can store your log files in your bucket for as long as you need to, but you can also define Amazon S3 lifecycle rules to archive or delete log files automatically. By default, your log files are encrypted by using Amazon S3 server-side encryption (SSE).

You can also aggregate Kinesis Data Streams log files from multiple AWS regions and multiple AWS accounts into a single Amazon S3 bucket. For information, see Aggregating CloudTrail Log Files to a Single Amazon S3 Bucket in the *AWS CloudTrail User Guide*.

You can have CloudTrail publish SNS notifications when new log files are delivered if you want to take quick action upon log file delivery. For information, see Configuring Amazon SNS Notifications in the *AWS CloudTrail*

Log File Entries for Kinesis Data Streams

CloudTrail log files can contain one or more log entries, where each entry is made up of multiple JSON-formatted events. A log entry represents a single request from any source and includes information about the requested action, any parameters, the date and time of the action, and so on. The log entries are not guaranteed to be in any particular order. That is, this is not an ordered stack trace of API calls.

The following is an example CloudTrail log entry.

```
1  {
2      "Records": [
3          {
4              "eventVersion": "1.01",
5              "userIdentity": {
6                  "type": "IAMUser",
7                  "principalId": "EX_PRINCIPAL_ID",
8                  "arn": "arn:aws:iam::012345678910:user/Alice",
9                  "accountId": "012345678910",
10                 "accessKeyId": "EXAMPLE_KEY_ID",
11                 "userName": "Alice"
12             },
13             "eventTime": "2014-04-19T00:16:31Z",
14             "eventSource": "kinesis.amazonaws.com",
15             "eventName": "CreateStream",
16             "awsRegion": "us-east-1",
17             "sourceIPAddress": "127.0.0.1",
18             "userAgent": "aws-sdk-java/unknown-version Linux/x.xx",
19             "requestParameters": {
20                 "shardCount": 1,
21                 "streamName": "GoodStream"
22             },
23             "responseElements": null,
24             "requestID": "db6c59f8-c757-11e3-bc3b-57923b443c1c",
25             "eventID": "b7acfcd0-6ca9-4ee1-a3d7-c4e8d420d99b"
26         },
27         {
28             "eventVersion": "1.01",
29             "userIdentity": {
30                 "type": "IAMUser",
31                 "principalId": "EX_PRINCIPAL_ID",
32                 "arn": "arn:aws:iam::012345678910:user/Alice",
33                 "accountId": "012345678910",
34                 "accessKeyId": "EXAMPLE_KEY_ID",
35                 "userName": "Alice"
36             },
37             "eventTime": "2014-04-19T00:17:06Z",
38             "eventSource": "kinesis.amazonaws.com",
39             "eventName": "DescribeStream",
40             "awsRegion": "us-east-1",
41             "sourceIPAddress": "127.0.0.1",
42             "userAgent": "aws-sdk-java/unknown-version Linux/x.xx",
43             "requestParameters": {
44                 "streamName": "GoodStream"
```

```
45          },
46          "responseElements": null,
47          "requestID": "f0944d86-c757-11e3-b4ae-25654b1d3136",
48          "eventID": "0b2f1396-88af-4561-b16f-398f8eaea596"
49      },
50      {
51          "eventVersion": "1.01",
52          "userIdentity": {
53              "type": "IAMUser",
54              "principalId": "EX_PRINCIPAL_ID",
55              "arn": "arn:aws:iam::012345678910:user/Alice",
56              "accountId": "012345678910",
57              "accessKeyId": "EXAMPLE_KEY_ID",
58              "userName": "Alice"
59          },
60          "eventTime": "2014-04-19T00:15:02Z",
61          "eventSource": "kinesis.amazonaws.com",
62          "eventName": "ListStreams",
63          "awsRegion": "us-east-1",
64          "sourceIPAddress": "127.0.0.1",
65          "userAgent": "aws-sdk-java/unknown-version Linux/x.xx",
66          "requestParameters": {
67              "limit": 10
68          },
69          "responseElements": null,
70          "requestID": "a68541ca-c757-11e3-901b-cbcfe5b3677a",
71          "eventID": "22a5fb8f-4e61-4bee-a8ad-3b72046b4c4d"
72      },
73      {
74          "eventVersion": "1.01",
75          "userIdentity": {
76              "type": "IAMUser",
77              "principalId": "EX_PRINCIPAL_ID",
78              "arn": "arn:aws:iam::012345678910:user/Alice",
79              "accountId": "012345678910",
80              "accessKeyId": "EXAMPLE_KEY_ID",
81              "userName": "Alice"
82          },
83          "eventTime": "2014-04-19T00:17:07Z",
84          "eventSource": "kinesis.amazonaws.com",
85          "eventName": "DeleteStream",
86          "awsRegion": "us-east-1",
87          "sourceIPAddress": "127.0.0.1",
88          "userAgent": "aws-sdk-java/unknown-version Linux/x.xx",
89          "requestParameters": {
90              "streamName": "GoodStream"
91          },
92          "responseElements": null,
93          "requestID": "f10cd97c-c757-11e3-901b-cbcfe5b3677a",
94          "eventID": "607e7217-311a-4a08-a904-ec02944596dd"
95      },
96      {
97          "eventVersion": "1.01",
98          "userIdentity": {
```

```
 99              "type": "IAMUser",
100              "principalId": "EX_PRINCIPAL_ID",
101              "arn": "arn:aws:iam::012345678910:user/Alice",
102              "accountId": "012345678910",
103              "accessKeyId": "EXAMPLE_KEY_ID",
104              "userName": "Alice"
105          },
106          "eventTime": "2014-04-19T00:15:03Z",
107          "eventSource": "kinesis.amazonaws.com",
108          "eventName": "SplitShard",
109          "awsRegion": "us-east-1",
110          "sourceIPAddress": "127.0.0.1",
111          "userAgent": "aws-sdk-java/unknown-version Linux/x.xx",
112          "requestParameters": {
113              "shardToSplit": "shardId-000000000000",
114              "streamName": "GoodStream",
115              "newStartingHashKey": "11111111"
116          },
117          "responseElements": null,
118          "requestID": "a6e6e9cd-c757-11e3-901b-cbcfe5b3677a",
119          "eventID": "dcd2126f-c8d2-4186-b32a-192dd48d7e33"
120      },
121      {
122          "eventVersion": "1.01",
123          "userIdentity": {
124              "type": "IAMUser",
125              "principalId": "EX_PRINCIPAL_ID",
126              "arn": "arn:aws:iam::012345678910:user/Alice",
127              "accountId": "012345678910",
128              "accessKeyId": "EXAMPLE_KEY_ID",
129              "userName": "Alice"
130          },
131          "eventTime": "2014-04-19T00:16:56Z",
132          "eventSource": "kinesis.amazonaws.com",
133          "eventName": "MergeShards",
134          "awsRegion": "us-east-1",
135          "sourceIPAddress": "127.0.0.1",
136          "userAgent": "aws-sdk-java/unknown-version Linux/x.xx",
137          "requestParameters": {
138              "streamName": "GoodStream",
139              "adjacentShardToMerge": "shardId-000000000002",
140              "shardToMerge": "shardId-000000000001"
141          },
142          "responseElements": null,
143          "requestID": "e9f9c8eb-c757-11e3-bf1d-6948db3cd570",
144          "eventID": "77cf0d06-ce90-42da-9576-71986fec411f"
145      }
146  ]
147 }
```

Monitoring the Kinesis Client Library with Amazon CloudWatch

The Kinesis Client Library (KCL) for Amazon Kinesis Data Streams publishes custom Amazon CloudWatch metrics on your behalf, using the name of your KCL application as the namespace. You can view these metrics by navigating to the CloudWatch console and choosing **Custom Metrics**. For more information about custom metrics, see Publish Custom Metrics in the *Amazon CloudWatch User Guide*.

There is a nominal charge for the metrics uploaded to CloudWatch by the KCL; specifically, *Amazon CloudWatch Custom Metrics* and *Amazon CloudWatch API Requests* charges apply. For more information, see Amazon CloudWatch Pricing.

Topics
- Metrics and Namespace
- Metric Levels and Dimensions
- Metric Configuration
- List of Metrics

Metrics and Namespace

The namespace used to upload metrics will be the application name specified when you launch the KCL.

Metric Levels and Dimensions

There are two options to control which metrics are uploaded to CloudWatch:

metric levels
Every metric is assigned an individual level. When you set a metrics reporting level, metrics with an individual level below the reporting level are not sent to CloudWatch. The levels are: NONE, SUMMARY, and DETAILED. The default setting is DETAILED; that is, all metrics are sent to CloudWatch. A reporting level of NONE means no metrics are sent at all. For information about which levels are assigned to what metrics, see List of Metrics.

enabled dimensions
Every KCL metric has associated dimensions that also get sent to CloudWatch. Operation dimension is always uploaded and cannot be disabled. By default, the WorkerIdentifier dimension is disabled, and only the Operation and ShardId dimensions are uploaded.
For more information about CloudWatch metric dimensions, see the Dimensions section in the CloudWatch Concepts topic, in the Amazon CloudWatch User Guide.
Note that when the WorkerIdentifier dimension is enabled, if a different value is used for the worker ID property every time a particular KCL worker restarts, new sets of metrics with new WorkerIdentifier dimension values are sent to CloudWatch. If you need the WorkerIdentifier dimension value to be the same across specific KCL worker restarts, you must explicitly specify the same worker ID value during initialization for each worker. Note that the worker ID value for each active KCL worker must be unique across all KCL workers.

Metric Configuration

Metric levels and enabled dimensions can be configured using the KinesisClientLibConfiguration instance, which is passed to Worker when launching the KCL application. In the MultiLangDaemon case, the metricsLevel and metricsEnabledDimensions properties can be specified in the .properties file used to launch the MultiLangDaemon KCL application.

Metric levels can be assigned one of three values: NONE, SUMMARY, or DETAILED. Enabled dimensions values must be comma-separated strings with the list of dimensions that are allowed for the CloudWatch metrics. The dimensions used by the KCL application are Operation, ShardId, and WorkerIdentifier.

List of Metrics

The following tables list the KCL metrics, grouped by scope and operation.

Topics

- Per-KCL-Application Metrics
- Per-Worker Metrics
- Per-Shard Metrics

Per-KCL-Application Metrics

These metrics are aggregated across all KCL workers within the scope of the application, as defined by the Amazon CloudWatch namespace.

Topics

- InitializeTask
- ShutdownTask
- ShardSyncTask
- BlockOnParentTask

InitializeTask

The `InitializeTask` operation is responsible for initializing the record processor for the KCL application. The logic for this operation includes getting a shard iterator from Kinesis Data Streams and initializing the record processor.

Metric	Description
KinesisDataFetcher.getIterator.Success	Number of successful `Get.ShardIterator` operations per KCL application. Metric level: Detailed Units: Count
KinesisDataFetcher.getIterator.Time	Time taken per `GetShardIterator` operation for the given KCL application. Metric level: Detailed Units: Milliseconds
RecordProcessor.initialize.Time	Time taken by the record processor's initialize method. Metric level: Summary Units: Milliseconds
Success	Number of successful record processor initializations. Metric level: Summary Units: Count
Time	Time taken by the KCL worker for the record processor initialization. Metric level: Summary Units: Milliseconds

ShutdownTask

The `ShutdownTask` operation initiates the shutdown sequence for shard processing. This can occur because a shard is split or merged, or when the shard lease is lost from the worker. In both cases, the record processor `shutdown()` function is invoked. New shards are also discovered in the case where a shard was split or merged, resulting in creation of one or two new shards.

Metric	Description
CreateLease.Success	Number of times that new child shards are successfully added into the KCL application DynamoDB table following parent shard shutdown. Metric level: Detailed Units: Count
CreateLease.Time	Time taken for adding new child shard information in the KCL application DynamoDB table. Metric level: Detailed Units: Milliseconds
UpdateLease.Success	Number of successful final checkpoints during the record processor shutdown. Metric level: Detailed Units: Count
UpdateLease.Time	Time taken by the checkpoint operation during the record processor shutdown. Metric level: Detailed Units: Milliseconds
RecordProcessor.shutdown.Time	Time taken by the record processor's shutdown method. Metric level: Summary Units: Milliseconds
Success	Number of successful shutdown tasks. Metric level: Summary Units: Count
Time	Time taken by the KCL worker for the shutdown task. Metric level: Summary Units: Milliseconds

ShardSyncTask

The `ShardSyncTask` operation discovers changes to shard information for the Kinesis data stream, so new shards can be processed by the KCL application.

Metric	Description
CreateLease.Success	Number of successful attempts to add new shard information into the KCL application DynamoDB table. Metric level: Detailed Units: Count
CreateLease.Time	Time taken for adding new shard information in the KCL application DynamoDB table. Metric level: Detailed Units: Milliseconds
Success	Number of successful shard sync operations. Metric level: Summary Units: Count
Time	Time taken for the shard sync operation. Metric level: Summary Units: Milliseconds

BlockOnParentTask

If the shard is split or merged with other shards, then new child shards are created. The `BlockOnParentTask` operation ensures that record processing for the new shards does not start until the parent shards are completely processed by the KCL.

Metric	Description
Success	Number of successful checks for parent shard completion . Metric level: Summary Units: Count

Metric	Description
Time	Time taken for parent shards completion. Metric level: Summary Unit: Milliseconds

Per-Worker Metrics

These metrics are aggregated across all record processors consuming data from a Kinesis data stream, such as an Amazon EC2 instance.

Topics

- RenewAllLeases
- TakeLeases

RenewAllLeases

The `RenewAllLeases` operation periodically renews shard leases owned by a particular worker instance.

Metric	Description
RenewLease.Success	Number of successful lease renewals by the worker. Metric level: Detailed Units: Count
RenewLease.Time	Time taken by the lease renewal operation. Metric level: Detailed Units: Milliseconds
CurrentLeases	Number of shard leases owned by the worker after all leases are renewed. Metric level: Summary Units: Count
LostLeases	Number of shard leases that were lost following an attempt to renew all leases owned by the worker. Metric level: Summary Units: Count
Success	Number of times lease renewal operation was successful for the worker. Metric level: Summary Units: Count
Time	Time taken for renewing all leases for the worker. Metric level: Summary Units: Milliseconds

TakeLeases

The `TakeLeases` operation balances record processing between all KCL workers. If the current KCL worker has fewer shard leases than required, it takes shard leases from another worker that is overloaded.

Metric	Description
ListLeases.Success	Number of times all shard leases were successfully retrieved from the KCL application DynamoDB table. Metric level: Detailed Units: Count
ListLeases.Time	Time taken to retrieve all shard leases from the KCL application DynamoDB table. Metric level: Detailed Units: Milliseconds

Metric	Description
TakeLease.Success	Number of times the worker successfully took shard leases from other KCL workers. Metric level: Detailed Units: Count
TakeLease.Time	Time taken to update the lease table with leases taken by the worker. Metric level: Detailed Units: Milliseconds
NumWorkers	Total number of workers, as identified by a specific worker. Metric level: Summary Units: Count
NeededLeases	Number of shard leases that the current worker needs for a balanced shard-processing load. Metric level: Detailed Units: Count
LeasesToTake	Number of leases that the worker will attempt to take. Metric level: Detailed Units: Count
TakenLeases	Number of leases taken successfully by the worker. Metric level: Summary Units: Count
TotalLeases	Total number of shards that the KCL application is processing. Metric level: Detailed Units: Count
ExpiredLeases	Total number of shards that are not being processed by any worker, as identified by the specific worker. Metric level: Summary Units: Count
Success	Number of times the `TakeLeases` operation successfully completed. Metric level: Summary Units: Count
Time	Time taken by the `TakeLeases` operation for a worker. Metric level: Summary Units: Milliseconds

Per-Shard Metrics

These metrics are aggregated across a single record processor.

ProcessTask

The `ProcessTask` operation calls GetRecords with the current iterator position to retrieve records from the stream and invokes the record processor `processRecords` function.

Metric	Description
KinesisDataFetcher.getRecords.Success	Number of successful `GetRecords` operations per Kinesis data stream shard. Metric level: Detailed Units: Count
KinesisDataFetcher.getRecords.Time	Time taken per `GetRecords` operation for the Kinesis data stream shard. Metric level: Detailed Units: Milliseconds
UpdateLease.Success	Number of successful checkpoints made by the record processor for the given shard. Metric level: Detailed Units: Count

Metric	Description
UpdateLease.Time	Time taken for each checkpoint operation for the given shard. Metric level: Detailed Units: Milliseconds
DataBytesProcessed	Total size of records processed in bytes on each `ProcessTask` invocation. Metric level: Summary Units: Byte
RecordsProcessed	Number of records processed on each `ProcessTask` invocation. Metric level: Summary Units: Count
ExpiredIterator	Number of ExpiredIteratorException received when calling `GetRecords`. Metric level: Summary Units: Count
MillisBehindLatest	Time that the current iterator is behind from the latest record (tip) in the shard. This value is less than or equal to the difference in time between the latest record in a response and the current time. This is a more accurate reflection of how far a shard is from the tip than comparing timestamps in the last response record. Note that this value applies to the latest batch of records, not an average of all timestamps in each record.Metric level: SummaryUnits: Milliseconds
RecordProcessor.processRecords.Time	Time taken by the record processor's `processRecords` method. Metric level: Summary Units: Milliseconds
Success	Number of successful process task operations. Metric level: Summary Units: Count
Time	Time taken for the process task operation. Metric level: Summary Units: Milliseconds

Monitoring the Kinesis Producer Library with Amazon CloudWatch

The Kinesis Producer Library (KPL) for Amazon Kinesis Data Streams publishes custom Amazon CloudWatch metrics on your behalf. You can view these metrics by navigating to the CloudWatch console and choosing **Custom Metrics**. For more information about custom metrics, see Publish Custom Metrics in the *Amazon CloudWatch User Guide*.

There is a nominal charge for the metrics uploaded to CloudWatch by the KPL; specifically, Amazon CloudWatch Custom Metrics and Amazon CloudWatch API Requests charges apply. For more information, see Amazon CloudWatch Pricing. Local metrics gathering does not incur CloudWatch charges.

Topics

- Metrics, Dimensions, and Namespaces
- Metric Level and Granularity
- Local Access and Amazon CloudWatch Upload
- List of Metrics

Metrics, Dimensions, and Namespaces

You can specify an application name when launching the KPL, which is then used as part of the namespace when uploading metrics. This is optional; the KPL provides a default value if an application name is not set.

You can also configure the KPL to add arbitrary additional dimensions to the metrics. This is useful if you want finer-grained data in your CloudWatch metrics. For example, you can add the host name as a dimension, which will then allow you to identify uneven load distributions across your fleet. All KPL configuration settings are immutable, so these additional dimensions cannot be changed after the KPL instance is initialized.

Metric Level and Granularity

There are two options to control the number of metrics uploaded to CloudWatch:

metric level
This is a rough gauge of how important a metric is. Every metric is assigned a level. When you set a level, metrics with levels below that are not sent to CloudWatch. The levels are NONE, SUMMARY, and DETAILED. The default setting is DETAILED; that is, all metrics. NONE means no metrics at all, so no metrics are actually assigned to that level.

granularity
This controls whether the same metric is emitted at additional levels of granularity. The levels are GLOBAL, STREAM, and SHARD. The default setting is SHARD, which contains the most granular metrics.
When SHARD is chosen, metrics are emitted with the stream name and shard ID as dimensions. In addition, the same metric is also emitted with only the stream name dimension, and the metric without the stream name. This means that, for a particular metric, two streams with two shards each will produce seven CloudWatch metrics: one for each shard, one for each stream, and one overall; all describing the same statistics but at different levels of granularity. For an illustration, see the diagram below.
The different granularity levels form a hierarchy, and all the metrics in the system form trees, rooted at the metric names:

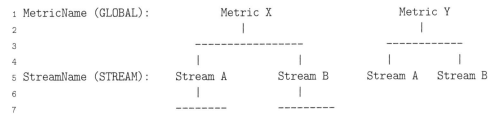

159

```
8                            |        |        |        |
9 ShardID (SHARD):      Shard 0 Shard 1  Shard 0 Shard 1
```

Not all metrics are available at the shard level; some are stream level or global by nature. These will not be produced at shard level even if you have enabled shard-level metrics (`Metric Y` in the diagram above).

When you specify an additional dimension, you need to provide values for `tuple:<DimensionName, DimensionValue, Granularity>`. The granularity is used to determine where the custom dimension is inserted in the hierarchy: `GLOBAL` means the additional dimension is inserted after the metric name, `STREAM` means it's inserted after the stream name, and `SHARD` means it's inserted after the shard ID. If multiple additional dimensions are given per granularity level, they are inserted in the order given.

Local Access and Amazon CloudWatch Upload

Metrics for the current KPL instance are available locally in real time; you can query the KPL at any time to get them. The KPL locally computes the sum, average, minimum, maximum, and count of every metric, as in CloudWatch.

You can get statistics that are cumulative from the start of the program to the present point in time, or using a rolling window over the past N seconds, where N is an integer between 1 and 60.

All metrics are available for upload to CloudWatch. This is especially useful for aggregating data across multiple hosts, monitoring, and alarming. This functionality is not available locally.

As described previously, you can select which metrics to upload with the *metric level* and *granularity* settings. Metrics that are not uploaded are available locally.

Uploading data points individually is untenable because it could produce millions of uploads per second, if traffic is high. For this reason, the KPL aggregates metrics locally into 1-minute buckets and uploads a statistics object to CloudWatch one time per minute, per enabled metric.

List of Metrics

Metric	Description
User Records Received	Count of how many logical user records were received by the KPL core for put operations. Not available at shard level. Metric level: Detailed Unit: Count
User Records Pending	Periodic sample of how many user records are currently pending. A record is pending if it is either currently buffered and waiting for to be sent, or sent and in-flight to the backend service. Not available at shard level. The KPL provides a dedicated method to retrieve this metric at the global level for customers to manage their put rate. Metric level: Detailed Unit: Count
User Records Put	Count of how many logical user records were put successfully. The KPL does not count failed records for this metric. This allows the average to give the success rate, the count to give the total attempts, and the difference between the count and sum to give the failure count. Metric level: Summary Unit: Count

160

Metric	Description
User Records Data Put	Bytes in the logical user records successfully put. Metric level: Detailed Unit: Bytes
Kinesis Records Put	Count of how many Kinesis Data Streams records were put successfully (each Kinesis Data Streams record can contain multiple user records). The KPL outputs a zero for failed records. This allows the average to give the success rate, the count to give the total attempts, and the difference between the count and sum to give the failure count. Metric level: Summary Unit: Count
Kinesis Records Data Put	Bytes in the Kinesis Data Streams records. Metric level: Detailed Unit: Bytes
Errors by Code	Count of each type of error code. This introduces an additional dimension of `ErrorCode`, in addition to the normal dimensions such as `StreamName` and `ShardId`. Not every error can be traced to a shard. The errors that cannot be traced are only emitted at stream or global levels. This metric captures information about such things as throttling, shard map changes, internal failures, service unavailable, timeouts, and so on. Kinesis Data Streams API errors are counted one time per Kinesis Data Streams record. Multiple user records within a Kinesis Data Streams record do not generate multiple counts. Metric level: Summary Unit: Count
All Errors	This is triggered by the same errors as **Errors by Code**, but does not distinguish between types. This is useful as a general monitor of the error rate without requiring a manual sum of the counts from all the different types of errors. Metric level: Summary Unit: Count
Retries per Record	Number of retries performed per user record. Zero is emitted for records that succeed in one try. Data is emitted at the moment a user record finishes (when it either succeeds or can no longer be retried). If record time-to-live is a large value, this metric may be significantly delayed. Metric level: Detailed Unit: Count
Buffering Time	The time between a user record arriving at the KPL and leaving for the backend. This information is transmitted back to the user on a per-record basis, but is also available as an aggregated statistic. Metric level: Summary Unit: Milliseconds
Request Time	The time it takes to perform `PutRecordsRequests`. Metric level: Detailed Unit: Milliseconds
User Records per Kinesis Record	The number of logical user records aggregated into a single Kinesis Data Streams record. Metric level: Detailed Unit: Count

Metric	Description
Amazon Kinesis Records per PutRecordsRequest	The number of Kinesis Data Streams records aggregated into a single `PutRecordsRequest`. Not available at shard level. Metric level: Detailed Unit: Count
User Records per PutRecordsRequest	The total number of user records contained within a `PutRecordsRequest`. This is roughly equivalent to the product of the previous two metrics. Not available at shard level. Metric level: Detailed Unit: Count

Tagging Your Streams in Amazon Kinesis Data Streams

You can assign your own metadata to streams you create in Amazon Kinesis Data Streams in the form of *tags*. A tag is a key-value pair that you define for a stream. Using tags is a simple yet powerful way to manage AWS resources and organize data, including billing data.

Topics

- Tag Basics
- Tracking Costs Using Tagging
- Tag Restrictions
- Tagging Streams Using the Kinesis Data Streams Console
- Tagging Streams Using the AWS CLI
- Tagging Streams Using the Kinesis Data Streams API

Tag Basics

You use the Kinesis Data Streams console, AWS CLI, or Kinesis Data Streams API to complete the following tasks:

- Add tags to a stream
- List the tags for your streams
- Remove tags from a stream

You can use tags to categorize your streams. For example, you can categorize streams by purpose, owner, or environment. Because you define the key and value for each tag, you can create a custom set of categories to meet your specific needs. For example, you might define a set of tags that helps you track streams by owner and associated application. Here are several examples of tags:

- Project: Project name
- Owner: Name
- Purpose: Load testing
- Application: Application name
- Environment: Production

Tracking Costs Using Tagging

You can use tags to categorize and track your AWS costs. When you apply tags to your AWS resources, including streams, your AWS cost allocation report includes usage and costs aggregated by tags. You can apply tags that represent business categories (such as cost centers, application names, or owners) to organize your costs across multiple services. For more information, see Use Cost Allocation Tags for Custom Billing Reports in the *AWS Billing and Cost Management User Guide*.

Tag Restrictions

The following restrictions apply to tags.

Basic restrictions

- The maximum number of tags per resource (stream) is 50.
- Tag keys and values are case-sensitive.
- You can't change or edit tags for a deleted stream.

Tag key restrictions

- Each tag key must be unique. If you add a tag with a key that's already in use, your new tag overwrites the existing key-value pair.
- You can't start a tag key with `aws:` because this prefix is reserved for use by AWS. AWS creates tags that begin with this prefix on your behalf, but you can't edit or delete them.
- Tag keys must be between 1 and 128 Unicode characters in length.
- Tag keys must consist of the following characters: Unicode letters, digits, white space, and the following special characters: `_ . / = + - @`.

Tag value restrictions

- Tag values must be between 0 and 255 Unicode characters in length.
- Tag values can be blank. Otherwise, they must consist of the following characters: Unicode letters, digits, white space, and any of the following special characters: `_ . / = + - @`.

Tagging Streams Using the Kinesis Data Streams Console

You can add, list, and remove tags using the Kinesis Data Streams console.

To view the tags for a stream

1. Open the Kinesis Data Streams console. In the navigation bar, expand the region selector and select a region.

2. On the **Stream List** page, select a stream.

3. On the **Stream Details** page, click the **Tags** tab.

To add a tag to a stream

1. Open the Kinesis Data Streams console. In the navigation bar, expand the region selector and select a region.

2. On the **Stream List** page, select a stream.

3. On the **Stream Details** page, click the **Tags** tab.

4. Specify the tag key in the **Key** field, optionally specify a tag value in the **Value** field, and then click **Add Tag**.

   If the **Add Tag** button is not enabled, either the tag key or tag value that you specified don't meet the tag restrictions. For more information, see Tag Restrictions.

5. To view your new tag in the list on the **Tags** tab, click the refresh icon.

To remove a tag from a stream

1. Open the Kinesis Data Streams console. In the navigation bar, expand the region selector and select a region.

2. On the Stream List page, select a stream.

3. On the Stream Details page, click the **Tags** tab, and then click the **Remove** icon for the tag.

4. In the **Delete Tag** dialog box, click **Yes, Delete**.

Tagging Streams Using the AWS CLI

You can add, list, and remove tags using the AWS CLI. For examples, see the following documentation.

add-tags-to-stream
Adds or updates tags for the specified stream.

list-tags-for-stream
Lists the tags for the specified stream.

remove-tags-from-stream
Removes tags from the specified stream.

Tagging Streams Using the Kinesis Data Streams API

You can add, list, and remove tags using the Kinesis Data Streams API. For examples, see the following documentation:

AddTagsToStream
Adds or updates tags for the specified stream.

ListTagsForStream
Lists the tags for the specified stream.

RemoveTagsFromStream
Removes tags from the specified stream.

Controlling Access to Amazon Kinesis Data Streams Resources Using IAM

AWS Identity and Access Management (IAM) enables you to do the following:

- Create users and groups under your AWS account
- Assign unique security credentials to each user under your AWS account
- Control each user's permissions to perform tasks using AWS resources
- Allow the users in another AWS account to share your AWS resources
- Create roles for your AWS account and define the users or services that can assume them
- Use existing identities for your enterprise to grant permissions to perform tasks using AWS resources

By using IAM with Kinesis Data Streams, you can control whether users in your organization can perform a task using specific Kinesis Data Streams API actions and whether they can use specific AWS resources.

If you are developing an application using the Kinesis Client Library (KCL), your policy must include permissions for Amazon DynamoDB and Amazon CloudWatch; the KCL uses DynamoDB to track state information for the application, and CloudWatch to send KCL metrics to CloudWatch on your behalf. For more information about the KCL, see Developing Amazon Kinesis Data Streams Consumers Using the Kinesis Client Library.

For more information about IAM, see the following:

- AWS Identity and Access Management (IAM)
- Getting Started
- IAM User Guide

For more information about IAM and Amazon DynamoDB, see Using IAM to Control Access to Amazon DynamoDB Resources in the *Amazon DynamoDB Developer Guide*.

For more information about IAM and Amazon CloudWatch, see Controlling User Access to Your AWS Account in the *Amazon CloudWatch User Guide*.

Topics

- Policy Syntax
- Actions for Kinesis Data Streams
- Amazon Resource Names (ARNs) for Kinesis Data Streams
- Example Policies for Kinesis Data Streams

Policy Syntax

An IAM policy is a JSON document that consists of one or more statements. Each statement is structured as follows:

```
1  {
2    "Statement":[{
3      "Effect":"effect",
4      "Action":"action",
5      "Resource":"arn",
6      "Condition":{
7        "condition":{
8          "key":"value"
9          }
10        }
11      }
12    ]
13  }
```

There are various elements that make up a statement:

- **Effect:** The *effect* can be `Allow` or `Deny`. By default, IAM users don't have permission to use resources and API actions, so all requests are denied. An explicit allow overrides the default. An explicit deny overrides any allows.
- **Action**: The *action* is the specific API action for which you are granting or denying permission.
- **Resource**: The resource that's affected by the action. To specify a resource in the statement, you need to use its Amazon Resource Name (ARN).
- **Condition**: Conditions are optional. They can be used to control when your policy will be in effect.

As you create and manage IAM policies, you might want to use the IAM Policy Generator and the IAM Policy Simulator.

Actions for Kinesis Data Streams

In an IAM policy statement, you can specify any API action from any service that supports IAM. For Kinesis Data Streams, use the following prefix with the name of the API action: `kinesis:`. For example: `kinesis:CreateStream`, `kinesis:ListStreams`, and `kinesis:DescribeStream`.

To specify multiple actions in a single statement, separate them with commas as follows:

```
1 "Action": ["kinesis:action1", "kinesis:action2"]
```

You can also specify multiple actions using wildcards. For example, you can specify all actions whose name begins with the word "Get" as follows:

```
1 "Action": "kinesis:Get*"
```

To specify all Kinesis Data Streams operations, use the * wildcard as follows:

```
1 "Action": "kinesis:*"
```

For the complete list of Kinesis Data Streams API actions, see the Amazon Kinesis API Reference.

Amazon Resource Names (ARNs) for Kinesis Data Streams

Each IAM policy statement applies to the resources that you specify using their ARNs.

Use the following ARN resource format for Kinesis data streams:

```
1 arn:aws:kinesis:region:account-id:stream/stream-name
```

For example:

```
1 "Resource": arn:aws:kinesis:*:111122223333:stream/my-stream
```

Example Policies for Kinesis Data Streams

The following example policies demonstrate how you could control user access to your Kinesis data streams.

Example 1: Allow users to get data from a stream
This policy allows a user or group to perform the `DescribeStream`, `GetShardIterator`, and `GetRecords` operations on the specified stream and `ListStreams` on any stream. This policy could be applied to users who should be able to get data from a specific stream.

```
 1  {
 2      "Version": "2012-10-17",
 3      "Statement": [
 4          {
 5              "Effect": "Allow",
 6              "Action": [
 7                  "kinesis:Get*",
 8                  "kinesis:DescribeStream"
 9              ],
10              "Resource": [
11                  "arn:aws:kinesis:us-east-1:111122223333:stream/stream1"
12              ]
13          },
14          {
15              "Effect": "Allow",
16              "Action": [
17                  "kinesis:ListStreams"
18              ],
19              "Resource": [
20                  "*"
21              ]
22          }
23      ]
24  }
```

Example 2: Allow users to add data to any stream in the account

This policy allows a user or group to use the `PutRecord` operation with any of the account's streams. This policy could be applied to users that should be able to add data records to all streams in an account.

```
 1  {
 2      "Version": "2012-10-17",
 3      "Statement": [
 4          {
 5              "Effect": "Allow",
 6              "Action": [
 7                  "kinesis:PutRecord"
 8              ],
 9              "Resource": [
10                  "arn:aws:kinesis:us-east-1:111122223333:stream/*"
11              ]
12          }
13      ]
14  }
```

Example 3: Allow any Kinesis Data Streams action on a specific stream

This policy allows a user or group to use any Kinesis Data Streams operation on the specified stream. This policy could be applied to users that should have administrative control over a specific stream.

```
 1  {
 2      "Version": "2012-10-17",
 3      "Statement": [
 4          {
 5              "Effect": "Allow",
 6              "Action": "kinesis:*",
 7              "Resource": [
 8                  "arn:aws:kinesis:us-east-1:111122223333:stream/stream1"
```

```
 9            ]
10        }
11    ]
12 }
```

Example 4: Allow any Kinesis Data Streams action on any stream

This policy allows a user or group to use any Kinesis Data Streams operation on any stream in an account. Because this policy grants full access to all your streams, you should restrict it to administrators only.

```
 1 {
 2     "Version": "2012-10-17",
 3     "Statement": [
 4         {
 5             "Effect": "Allow",
 6             "Action": "kinesis:*",
 7             "Resource": [
 8                 "arn:aws:kinesis:*:111122223333:stream/*"
 9             ]
10         }
11     ]
12 }
```

Using Amazon Kinesis Data Streams with Interface VPC Endpoints

Interface VPC endpoints for Kinesis Data Streams

You can use an interface VPC endpoint to keep traffic between your Amazon VPC and Kinesis Data Streams from leaving the Amazon network. Interface VPC endpoints don't require an internet gateway, NAT device, VPN connection, or AWS Direct Connect connection. Interface VPC endpoints are powered by AWS PrivateLink, an AWS technology that enables private communication between AWS services using an elastic network interface with private IPs in your Amazon VPC. For more information, see Amazon Virtual Private Cloud.

Using interface VPC endpoints for Kinesis Data Streams

To get started you do not need to change the settings for your streams, producers, or consumers. Simply create an interface VPC endpoint in order for your Kinesis Data Streams traffic from and to your Amazon VPC resources to start flowing through the interface VPC endpoint.

The Kinesis Producer Library (KPL) and Kinesis Consumer Library (KCL) call AWS services like Amazon CloudWatch and Amazon DynamoDB using either public endpoints or private interface VPC endpoints, whichever are in use. For example, if your KPL application is running in a VPC with DynamoDB interface VPC endpoints enabled, calls between DynamoDB and your KCL application flow through the interface VPC endpoint.

Availability

Interface VPC endpoints are currently supported within the following regions:

- US East (Ohio)
- US East (N. Virginia)
- US West (Oregon)
- Asia Pacific (Tokyo)
- EU (Ireland)
- EU (Paris)

Using Server-Side Encryption

Server-side encryption using AWS Key Management Service (AWS KMS) keys makes it easy for you to meet strict data management requirements by encrypting your data at rest within Amazon Kinesis Data Streams.

Topics

- What Is Server-Side Encryption for Kinesis Streams?
- Costs, Regions, and Performance Considerations
- How Do I Get Started with Server-Side Encryption?
- Creating and Using User-Generated KMS Master Keys
- Permissions to Use User-Generated KMS Master Keys
- Verifying and Troubleshooting KMS Key Permissions

What Is Server-Side Encryption for Kinesis Streams?

Server-side encryption is a feature in Amazon Kinesis Data Streams that automatically encrypts data before it's at rest by using an AWS KMS customer master key (CMK) you specify. Data is encrypted before it's written to the Kinesis stream storage layer, and decrypted after it's retrieved from storage. As a result, your data is encrypted at rest within the Kinesis Data Streams service. This allows you to meet strict regulatory requirements and enhance the security of your data.

With server-side encryption, your Kinesis stream producers and consumers don't need to manage master keys or cryptographic operations. Your data is automatically encrypted as it enters and leaves the Kinesis Data Streams service, so your data at rest is encrypted. AWS KMS provides all the master keys that are used by the server-side encryption feature. AWS KMS makes it easy to use a CMK for Kinesis that is managed by AWS, a user-specified AWS KMS CMK, or a master key imported into the AWS KMS service.

Note
Server-side encryption encrypts incoming data only after encryption is enabled. Preexisting data in an unencrypted stream is not encrypted after server-side encryption is enabled.

Costs, Regions, and Performance Considerations

When you apply server-side encryption, you are subject to AWS KMS API usage and key costs. Unlike custom KMS master keys, the (Default) `aws/kinesis` customer master key (CMK) is offered free of charge. However, you still must pay for the API usage costs that Amazon Kinesis Data Streams incurs on your behalf.

API usage costs apply for every CMK, including custom ones. Kinesis Data Streams calls AWS KMS approximately every five minutes when it is rotating the data key. In a 30-day month, the total cost of AWS KMS API calls that are initiated by a Kinesis stream should be less than a few dollars. This cost scales with the number of user credentials that you use on your data producers and consumers because each user credential requires a unique API call to AWS KMS. When you use an IAM role for authentication, each assume role call results in unique user credentials. To save KMS costs, you might want to cache user credentials that are returned by the assume role call.

The following describes the costs by resource:

Keys

- The CMK for Kinesis that's managed by AWS (alias = `aws/kinesis`) is free.
- User-generated KMS keys are subject to KMS key costs. For more information, see AWS Key Management Service Pricing.

KMS API Usage

For every encrypted stream, the Kinesis service calls the AWS KMS service approximately every five minutes to create a new data encryption key. In a 30-day month, each encrypted stream generates approximately 8,640 KMS API requests. API requests to generate new data encryption keys are subject to AWS KMS usage costs. For more information, see AWS Key Management Service Pricing: Usage.

Availability of Server-Side Encryption by Region

Server-side encryption of Kinesis streams is available in the following regions.

Region Name	Region
US East (Ohio)	us-east-2
US East (N. Virginia)	us-east-1
US West (Oregon)	us-west-2
US West (N. California)	us-west-1
AWS GovCloud (US)	us-gov-west-1
Canada (Central)	ca-central-1
EU (Ireland)	eu-west-1
EU (London)	eu-west-2
EU (Frankfurt)	eu-central-1
Asia Pacific (Tokyo) Region	ap-northeast-1
Asia Pacific (Seoul) Region	ap-northeast-2
Asia Pacific (Singapore)	ap-southeast-1
Asia Pacific (Mumbai)	ap-south-1
Asia Pacific (Sydney)	ap-southeast-2
South America (São Paulo)	sa-east-1

Performance Considerations

Due to the service overhead of applying encryption, applying server-side encryption will increase the typical latency of `PutRecord`, `PutRecords`, and `GetRecords` by less than 100s.

How Do I Get Started with Server-Side Encryption?

The easiest way to get started with server-side encryption is to use the AWS Management Console and the Amazon Kinesis KMS Service Key, `aws/kinesis`.

The following procedure demonstrates how to enable server-side encryption for a Kinesis stream.

To enable server-side encryption for a Kinesis stream

1. Sign in to the AWS Management Console and open the Amazon Kinesis Data Streams console.

2. Create or select a Kinesis stream in the AWS Management Console.

3. Choose the **details** tab.

4. In **Server-side encryption**, choose **edit**.

5. Unless you want to use a user-generated KMS master key, ensure the **(Default) aws/kinesis** KMS master key is selected. This is the KMS master key generated by the Kinesis service. Choose **Enabled**, and then choose **Save. Note**
   The default Kinesis service master key is free, however, the API calls made by Kinesis to the AWS KMS service are subject to KMS usage costs.

6. The stream transitions through a "pending" state. Once the stream returns to an "active" state with encryption enabled, all incoming data written to the stream is encrypted using the KMS master key you selected.

7. To disable server-side encryption, choose **Disabled** in **Server-side encryption** in the AWS Management Console, and then choose **Save**.

Creating and Using User-Generated KMS Master Keys

This section describes how to create and use your own KMS master keys, instead of using the master key administered by Amazon Kinesis.

Creating User-Generated KMS Master Keys

For instructions on creating your own master keys, see Creating Keys in the *AWS Key Management Service Developer Guide*. After you create keys for your account, the Kinesis Data Streams service returns these keys in the **KMS master key** list.

Using User-Generated KMS Master Keys

Once the correct permissions are applied to your consumers, producers, and administrators, you can use custom KMS master keys in your own AWS account or another AWS account. All KMS master keys in your account appear in the **KMS Master Key** list within the AWS Management Console.

To use custom KMS master keys located in another account, you need permissions to use those keys. You must also specify the ARN of the KMS master key in the ARN input box in the AWS Management Console.

Permissions to Use User-Generated KMS Master Keys

Before you can use server-side encryption with a user-generated KMS master key, you must configure AWS KMS key policies to allow encryption of streams and encryption and decryption of stream records. For examples and more information about AWS KMS permissions, see AWS KMS API Permissions: Actions and Resources Reference.

Note

The use of the default service key for encryption does not require application of custom IAM permissions.

Before you use user-generated KMS master keys, ensure that your Kinesis stream producers and consumers (IAM principals) are users in the KMS master key policy. Otherwise, writes and reads from a stream will fail, which could ultimately result in data loss, delayed processing, or hung applications. You can manage permissions for KMS keys using IAM policies. For more information, see Using IAM Policies with AWS KMS.

Example Producer Permissions

Your Kinesis stream producers must have the `kms:GenerateDataKey` permission.

```
1  {
2    "Version": "2012-10-17",
3    "Statement": [
4      {
5        "Effect": "Allow",
6        "Action": [
7          "kms:GenerateDataKey"
8        ],
9        "Resource": "arn:aws:kms:us-west-2:123456789012:key/1234abcd-12ab-34cd-56ef-1234567890ab
            "
10     },
11     {
12       "Effect": "Allow",
13       "Action": [
14         "kinesis:PutRecord",
15         "kinesis:PutRecords"
16       ],
17       "Resource": "arn:aws:kinesis:*:123456789012:MyStream"
18     }
19   ]
20 }
```

Example Consumer Permissions

Your Kinesis stream consumers must have the `kms:Decrypt` permission.

```
1  {
2    "Version": "2012-10-17",
3    "Statement": [
4      {
5        "Effect": "Allow",
6        "Action": [
7          "kms:Decrypt"
8        ],
```

```
 9          "Resource": "arn:aws:kms:us-west-2:123456789012:key/1234abcd-12ab-34cd-56ef-1234567890ab
               "
10      },
11      {
12          "Effect": "Allow",
13          "Action": [
14              "kinesis:GetRecords",
15              "kinesis:DescribeStream"
16          ],
17          "Resource": "arn:aws:kinesis:*:123456789012:MyStream"
18      }
19    ]
20  }
```

Amazon Kinesis Data Analytics and AWS Lambda use roles to consume Kinesis streams. Make sure to add the kms:Decrypt permission to the roles that these consumers use.

Stream Administrator Permissions

Kinesis stream administrators must have authorization to call kms:List* and "'kms:DescribeKey*'.

Verifying and Troubleshooting KMS Key Permissions

After enabling encryption on a Kinesis stream, we recommend that you monitor the success of your `putRecord`, `putRecords`, and `getRecords` calls using the following Amazon CloudWatch metrics:

- `PutRecord.Success`
- `PutRecords.Success`
- `GetRecords.Success`

Document History

The following table describes the important changes to the Amazon Kinesis Data Streams documentation.

Change	Description	Date Changed
New content for Server Side Encryption.	Added Using Server-Side Encryption.	July 7, 2017
New content for enhanced CloudWatch metrics.	Updated Monitoring Amazon Kinesis Data Streams.	April 19, 2016
New content for enhanced Kinesis agent.	Updated Writing to Amazon Kinesis Data Streams Using Kinesis Agent.	April 11, 2016
New content for using Kinesis agents.	Added Writing to Amazon Kinesis Data Streams Using Kinesis Agent.	October 2, 2015
Update KPL content for release 0.10.0.	Added Developing Amazon Kinesis Data Streams Producers Using the Kinesis Producer Library.	July 15, 2015
Update KCL metrics topic for configurable metrics.	Added Monitoring the Kinesis Client Library with Amazon CloudWatch.	July 9, 2015
Re-organized content.	Significantly re-organized content topics for more concise tree view and more logical grouping.	July 01, 2015
New KPL developer's guide topic.	Added Developing Amazon Kinesis Data Streams Producers Using the Kinesis Producer Library.	June 02, 2015
New KCL metrics topic.	Added Monitoring the Kinesis Client Library with Amazon CloudWatch.	May 19, 2015
Support for KCL .NET	Added Developing a Kinesis Client Library Consumer in .NET.	May 1, 2015
Support for KCL Node.js	Added Developing a Kinesis Client Library Consumer in Node.js.	March 26, 2015
Support for KCL Ruby	Added links to KCL Ruby library.	January 12, 2015
New API PutRecords	Added information about new PutRecords API to Adding Multiple Records with PutRecords.	December 15, 2014
Support for tagging	Added Tagging Your Streams in Amazon Kinesis Data Streams.	September 11, 2014
New CloudWatch metric	Added the metric GetRecords.IteratorAgeMilliseconds to Amazon Kinesis Data Streams Dimensions and Metrics.	September 3, 2014

Change	Description	Date Changed
New monitoring chapter	Added Monitoring Amazon Kinesis Data Streams and Monitoring the Amazon Kinesis Data Streams Service with Amazon CloudWatch.	July 30, 2014
New sample application	Added Tutorial: Visualizing Web Traffic Using Amazon Kinesis Data Streams.	June 27, 2014
Default shard limit	Updated the Amazon Kinesis Data Streams Limits: the default shard limit has been raised from 5 to 10.	February 25, 2014
Default shard limit	Updated the Amazon Kinesis Data Streams Limits: the default shard limit has been raised from 2 to 5.	January 28, 2014
API version updates	Updates for version 2013-12-02 of the Kinesis Data Streams API.	December 12, 2013
Initial release	Initial release of the Amazon Kinesis Developer Guide.	November 14, 2013

AWS Glossary

For the latest AWS terminology, see the AWS Glossary in the *AWS General Reference*.

www.ingramcontent.com/pod-product-compliance
Lightning Source LLC
LaVergne TN
LVHW082038050326
832904LV00005B/232